For my beloved gran, Mary Dale,
who made her transition to Spirit
during the writing of this book.

CONTENTS

LIST OF ACTIVATIONS

FOREWORD

My first introduction to the spirit world was when I was a teenager.

My mum suffered from depression when I was a child, following the birth of my youngest sister. It began as post-natal depression that wasn't effectively treated and worsened over the next year or so. At one point, she was quite unwell and was bedridden.

One night during this time, my mum opened her eyes to see her dad (my papa) standing at the foot of her bed, smiling warmly at her. He was like a photographic negative, semi-transparent, mum later explained. He spoke to her with the words 'Everything is going to be OK.' The following night her mum appeared, also offering reassurance. Papa had passed away a year earlier; granny, a year before then.

Mum didn't tell anyone for a few years, lest they questioned her sanity, given that she was suffering from depression at the time. But it was a completely real experience.

Recognizing my growing interest in the paranormal in my teenage years, other than my dad, I was the first person Mum shared this with. Learning of my mum's personal experience made the idea of spirit communication all the more real to me.

My interest has grown over the years such that I have personally written on some aspects of the paranormal, including the possibility that consciousness is not confined to the brain but that it's universal.

Reading *The Medium in Manolos* reminds us that we all have mediumship abilities to one degree or another. Through her lucid language, Lauren offers a step-by-step guide for developing our own abilities. She also teaches us that spirit can communicate in a multitude of ways.

It reminded me of a number of communications I received from my dog, Oscar, after he passed into the Spirit World in 2014. We were extremely close. Through Oscar, I came to understand what people meant when they described the loving bond we can have with animals. During the days following his passing, I received several indications that he was still around me.

The timing of his life was a sign in itself. He arrived in my life exactly two days before I began working on my book *I Heart Me: The Science of Self-Love*, and passed away exactly two days before I handed the final draft to my publisher. I learned more about self-love from Oscar than from any book I'd ever read, talk I'd ever listened to or any other experience I'd had. I was left in no doubt that he came into my life to help me, perhaps even to save me. I believe that he left when the job he came to do was done. Somehow, that helped me to deal with the pain of losing him.

While reading this book, I was reflecting on many of the signs he sent me. One, in particular, was exceptionally clear. I was driving on the motorway on the day of a lunar eclipse and had pulled over into motorway services so that I could enjoy the experience.

☆ x ☆

I held up my phone and recorded a short video of part of the eclipse. Later, while watching the video, I was astonished to see, in perfect clarity, Oscar's face holding a stick in his mouth. There was no mistaking it. Others could see it, too.

I stopped reading this book to find the video and watched it again several times, marvelling at the image of Oscar smiling back at me. Now it's one of my most treasured videos.

I decided to take a short break before reading the next few chapters and opened the Twitter app on my iPhone. Right there in my immediate Twitter feed was a photo of a person with 'Oscar' emblazoned on his chest in bold, capital letters. I simply smiled and thanked Oscar for still being an important presence in my life.

Lauren Robertson teaches us that we shouldn't ignore signs like these as random chance and simply dismiss them, but instead view them as genuine communications from our deceased loved ones. It's through acknowledging and trusting communications that we develop our mediumship abilities.

Lauren writes in a down-to-earth style that is both humorous and, at times, astonishingly real as she shares some of her own personal struggles. It takes courage as a teacher to admit your own perceived failings, but Lauren does so in such a way that encourages others to be honest with their own selves, too. It's through this honesty that we're better able to develop more self-love, which makes us more rounded individuals and better able to tap into our latent abilities.

Lauren has a degree in English literature and philosophy. This has certainly influenced her writing. At times, I felt like I was reading a novel that I couldn't put down. At other times, I was taken aback by the extraordinary clarity with which she puts forth her ideas of how mediumship works.

In Chapter 6, she proposes that mediumship abilities have evolved by natural selection, and argues that ability is related to empathy. She then refers to mediumship as 'phenomenological empathy'. I love that term. It appeals to me as a scientist and philosopher.

I first met Lauren at Glasgow's SECC (Scottish Exhibition and Conference Centre). I had spoken at a Hay House's 'I Can Do It!' conference and Lauren had joined the book-signing queue. When she reached the front, she asked if she could send me a few chapters of a book she was writing. Normally I wouldn't have time to do this, but there was something about Lauren – in the way she communicated, in the brightness of her eyes and her whole being that cried out I should read it. As she walked away, Michelle Pilley, the MD of Hay House UK, who was standing next to me at the time, leaned across and whispered, 'Can you send it to me too?' Michelle also saw something special in Lauren.

I believe that the book you're currently holding in your hands was always supposed to be read, and I feel gently satisfied that I was able to play a small part in the process by being a bridge that enabled Lauren to communicate with our publisher.

I hope it helps you to develop your own communication abilities.

David R. Hamilton PhD
Author of *I Heart Me: The Science of Self-Love*

INTRODUCTION

The idea for *The Medium in Manolos* arrived whilst I was in the shower, covered in suds. I wanted to write a book about mediumship that was contemporary, fresh and innovative, building on the insights and practices of the mediums who came before me, and adding something new besides. I was inspired to write it because, time and again, my clients, students and colleagues felt that developing their abilities through religion didn't resonate with them, and they were looking for a different approach that would both nourish them and deepen their connection with Spirit. What often came up in our conversations was the question: what next? Besides learning the basics of Spirit communication and getting a lot of practice, my fellow mediums were hungry to do more – to *learn* more – to take their mediumship to the next level. And it became clear to me over time that the next level involved overcoming the fear and self-doubt that often prevent mediums from fully stepping into their most miraculous work with Spirit. It seemed that a book was needed to clarify, elevate and strengthen the *mind* of the medium. I had practised mediumship one to one and on platforms all over the world for many years; I had completed an English

Literature and Philosophy degree that focused on the mind; and I had trained as a transformational coach specializing in healing limiting beliefs. So Spirit and I agreed, that day in the shower, that I was the right person to write such a book. And so, *The Medium in Manolos* was born.

The Medium in Manolos is a manual of confidence. My hope is that, if you are grieving, you will find ideas in these pages that will help you to grieve confidently, and inspire you to embrace your feelings so that they can be healed. I also hope that, if you are developing your mediumship, you will find tools and ideas here to help you overcome your fears and limiting beliefs, and instil within you the confidence to do truly transformational work with Spirit.

The Medium in Manolos is designed to be of value to anyone who has an interest in the practice of Spirit communication. Whether you wish to explore the possibility that a passed loved one is still present in your life, or you're a new medium who wants to create a healthy, powerful and confident foundation as you develop your gifts or you're an experienced medium who's looking for a new medium-centric approach to deepen your connection, there's something in these pages written, with love, for you.

The chapters in the book chart key moments in my mediumship journey: I begin as a grieving and devastated teenager, following the death of a beloved family member, and I evolve into a confident psychic medium working with amazing clients (here, and in Spirit) with whom miracles are created. As I advance, I extract my biggest takeaways, deepest lessons and most profound moments of clarity, offering them to you in the hope that they will help you to develop your own practice as a medium. Each chapter is designed to deepen your understanding of the relationship between your mind and the Mind of Spirit – my intention is that they will guide you towards stronger, more loving and more compelling impressions of people in Spirit. At the end of each chapter, I provide you with challenging and thought-provoking exercises that will enable you to apply the information explored.

Through the process of writing *The Medium in Manolos*, I have learned just how powerful Spirit communication can be, and how deeply we can touch someone's life with our mediumship. In a world where much blood is shed over our differences, I believe that mediumship has the power to remind us that we are all connected – and that we remain meaningfully connected to our loved ones who are no longer physically with us. When we allow the personality and love of a person in Spirit to move through us, we not only touch the person receiving the message, we change the lives of their family and friends, and those of the people *they* come into contact with. In this way, message by message, we can change the world.

If I'm honest, writing this book has been one of the hardest things I've ever done in my life. I wanted to write something that would make use of my forays into consciousness studies and analytic philosophy, whilst being a fun, entertaining and warm read, so that you would find it both thought-provoking and enjoyable. I wanted to write a book on the absolute cutting edge of mediumship development techniques, yet stay respectful of the approaches that have come before me. I wanted to write words that would comfort you if you are in the bitterest and darkest stages of grief or help deepen your connection with Spirit if you're a platform medium with a world tour and five books under your belt. Meeting all these needs was a challenge I could not have met, even in part, without many ruminative walks in the park, bursts of inspiration at 3 a.m. and litres upon litres of cappuccino.

Another thing that made producing this book difficult was that my beloved gran died during the writing process. She had been ill in hospital for six months, and I'd visited her every week, returning home to write about the celebration of eternal life, whilst she lay dying. When she passed away, I was nearing the end of the book, and I felt I could keep it together to finish it. I was doing OK, until one day, during a shopping trip in Glasgow city centre, I found myself walking behind a woman whose hair was styled exactly like my gran's, and who was wearing the same purple fleece gilet I'd often caressed when hugging her. I wanted to reach out and touch the woman, to feel that fleece-y softness one more time, but I couldn't. I cried so hard that day. It took me a while to put fingers to keys again after that.

In one way, it was a blessing that my gran died when she did. The first draft of this book was very high-vibe – too high-vibe, I thought, considering it was about the transition of our loved ones from physical life to death. My gran's passing helped me to reconnect with the raw love, and the pain of being bereft that makes us human, that makes us grieve. This prompted a more down-to-earth, compassionate rewrite of several chapters, which transformed the text you're about to read for the better.

Now that *The Medium in Manolos* is complete, I'm filled with so much gratitude. I hope that you will gain much from my experiences and insights as a teenage and 20-something medium, who has, at once, savoured every moment of exploring and celebrating the end of physical life, and stood in awe before the intimate expansiveness of life-eternal.

To make the most of this book, I encourage you to do the exercises or 'activations'. I have called them 'activations' because the first time I felt a person in Spirit draw close to me I experienced the sensation that some aspect of myself that had previously lain dormant had become activated. I have carefully chosen these exercises in the hope that you will experience that sensation too. Many of them, including the meditations, will give you the greatest benefit if you do them more than once. Repetition is said to be the mother of mastery, and when it comes to developing your awareness of Spirit in the ways I present, that is most definitely the case.

Also, many times throughout this book, I will ask you to use a journal – to write something, answer questions or complete exercises in it. I recommend, then, that you procure for yourself a journal – a gorgeous one that you'll want to write in – and that you sanctify and dedicate it to recording your expanding awareness of Spirit.

And finally... I'm going to ask you questions, evoke certain thoughts and ask you to consider certain things which may seem to have nothing to do with connecting with your loved ones in Spirit or developing your mediumship. But the questions and thoughts I'm going to ask you to consider occupy your conscious or subconscious mind, and throughout this book, we will be in the business of changing your mind about certain things. So even if you're not immediately sure why you're being asked to do something, please take it in good faith that every single exercise in this book has helped me, my clients and my students to develop our mediumship. This is all good stuff with no filler. Be honest, transparent and engaged with yourself throughout the process, follow the work faithfully and it will all click into place.

Changing the way we've always done things can be difficult, but if we want different results, we have to take different actions. Stick with the changes you decide to make for yourself and embrace the process. It's OK if it takes more than one attempt to make a new thought, action or behaviour stick. This book is not a test. You cannot fail. Take your time to grow, learn, back- and sidestep – that's not failure; that's called dancing.

All that remains now is for me to thank you for choosing me, and this book that I've written, as guides on your precious journey from, through and back around to Spirit. And now I'd like to invite you to begin that journey with me in Chapter 1, as we go back in time to a pivotal moment in my life.

CHAPTER 1

VALENTINE'S DAY

'I have to go see her immediately. If you don't take me, I'll walk by myself.' Some kind of firmness in my words told my mum I was serious. It was 10 p.m. and we were in our pyjamas, it was pitch black and lashing with rain outside. She looked doubtful and irritated.

'OK, I'll take you,' she said.

We bundled ourselves into the car and drove across town, to where my beloved gran, who'd bravely lived with breast cancer for years, was being tended by my aunt, a nurse. I'd received a phone call from my uncle moments before our car ride, and I knew by the tone of his voice that he didn't want to alarm me, but that something was very wrong. The urge to go to my gran was overwhelming, hence my insistence, and my mum, being equally intuitive, must have sensed it too.

I cracked my grandmother's bedroom door open slightly and peered in, searching for my father, unsure whether to enter as the relationship between us had grown painfully distant and awkward. He wasn't there.

My aunt and uncle sat by the bed, and for a moment, I couldn't see my gran, owing to just how incredibly fragile and transparent she'd become – she reminded me of a moth's wing. I sat down and held her tiny hand. She was unconscious, and I, being 17 and unable to be anything but myself with her, was cracking jokes and talking about good times – trying to bring her some cheer.

'Remember that time we were watching the snooker in silence and suddenly, out of nowhere, you said, "He's not got a snowball's chance in Hell of winning this." Oh, how we buckled and laughed for minutes at that comment – never really knowing why it was funny.'

She squeezed my hand.

Imperceptible to anyone but me – I felt it. I knew she could hear me. That squeeze told me she knew I was there. She knew how much I cared.

Mum and I sat in silence on the car ride home. I went to bed, switched off the light and cried myself to sleep.

I awoke the next morning to a crisp, cold, frosty Valentine's Day. I felt lighter, brighter – released from the smog of grief I'd disappeared into the night before. I got dressed and went downstairs. My mum was standing waiting for me, looking sombre.

'Your Gran Robertson passed away during the night.'

'I know,' I replied, having sensed that the lightness of my mind was connected to the end of her struggle.

My gran was the first person to really turn my face, heart and mind towards the Spirit World. When she died, her absence was painful, and yet the strength of the love I continued to feel between us made me feel that she was still around, somehow.

Gran Robertson watches over me still, and I feel her presence in my life every day. Just the other week (13 years after her passing), I commented to my mum on how sad it was that I didn't have any photographs of my gran – getting pictures wasn't possible, given the strained relationship with my dad. Imagine my surprise, then, when a few days later, a message notification popped up on social media from my mum, and all it contained was a scanned photograph of my gran and me. My mum had hired someone to clean out her house and sell some of her clothes and bags online. Several days after she handed over hundreds of items, the seller e-mailed Mum saying that she'd found this photograph hidden in the lining of one of her handbags.

Thanks, Gran.

I often think back to how I felt the day my gran died because, as a psychic medium for over 13 years, I've experienced such joy, so many miracles and such laughter with people's loved ones in Spirit that it can be easy for me to forget that the Divine and miraculous messages mean that someone you love has died. Thinking about Gran Mamie (my other name for her) reminds me of those feelings, and the care and respect with which I need to handle your emotions throughout this book.

Whether you are bereaved and experiencing the rawness of grief while you search for a way to heal, or you are a medium looking to develop your capacity for communication and to understand your relationship to Spirit more deeply, death touches us all, and our loved ones who have returned to the light – our family and friends in Spirit – have much to teach us.

So in this first chapter, I'd like to begin by exploring grief, and looking at some of the ways you can heal from it and reconnect with your loved ones who have passed, not as a medium, but as a loving human being who has gone through an intimate loss. I aim to help you lean into the intense, painful emotions you've experienced as a result of their leaving. I want to go there with you for your benefit – not because I believe your loved ones are dead and gone for ever (if I did, this would be a short book), but because coming to terms with their departure and being genuinely some way towards OK with it is the first step to kindling a relationship of a different sort with them – one which, although nonphysical, can yield much love, knowledge and healing, if you're available for it.

Whilst I have deep sympathy for the sadness you've gone through because a beloved person is no longer physically in your life, I should prepare you for the fact that this chapter will be the first and last time I refer to 'death' in a funereal, final-goodbye, sombre, Western, depressing, black-clad context. In the chapters to come, death will not be viewed as something to be sad about or fearful of – it will be referred to as a transcendent, ethereal celebration of life, and I invite you to make that leap with me. I will refer to your loved ones who've passed with some humour, a little fondness and a whole lot of life. And I hope that in sharing my joyful experience of communing with people who've passed away, you'll develop the ability – whether as griever, medium or both – to feel it too.

Love and Loss

When my gran died, I was absolutely devastated. She represented unconditional love to me, and when she was no longer here physically, I felt that my experience of love had massively diminished. Everything looked a little more grey and felt a little less meaningful, and nothing much seemed worth getting excited about.

You may have the idea that mediums don't grieve deeply over loss because they don't believe in it, but I'm here to tell you that the abilities of some of the best mediums were born of that very feeling. Great mediumship emerges when someone has loved very deeply, grieved very bitterly and realized that when the storm of grief has passed, the love they shared with the person who died is still standing. There are many roads to being a great medium, and this is definitely one of them.

The journey that has brought you to reading this book most probably comprises some distinctive steps: you have grieved, you are in search of a spiritual approach to healing grief, you have somehow felt the presence of your loved ones around you and you want to explore and understand how this could be, and what it means.

If you are reading this from a place of shock following a loss, or you're grieving or a lot of pain still remains over a loved one who may have passed a long time ago, be patient with yourself. There is no right or wrong way to grieve. There is no rule dictating when you have to get over it. Your world has been shattered and your heart broken. So let it be shattered, and let it be broken. Yes, you are Spirit. Spirit is in all beings, and all beings are connected as one through their shared spiritual nature. We do not become Spirit when we die. We are always Spirit. As a spiritual being, there is a part of you that is eternal, loving and powerful; but you are also human, and to be human is to feel pain, to be emotional and to grieve. So don't rush yourself to heal or beat yourself up. Don't think that anyone else's grief is more worthy than yours or compare how you are doing to how anyone else is doing. Don't hang on to the good days or fear the bad days, since both will pass – just let them.

Be angry. Get pissed off with Spirit. Say 'no' to seeing family or say 'yes' – whatever feels most kind to yourself. Drop the guilt. There's nothing you could've done differently, and whether you were there or not at the death was decided a long, long time ago, and not by you. Be fine with it, if you really are fine with it, and be devastated if you really are devastated. If the grief is ongoing, let it be ongoing, and if it's done – let it be done.

No one in Spirit requires you to hold a painful vigil for them. And, in fact, it is your love and joy that draw them closer, not your pain and suffering. When the pain is ready to leave, let it leave, and you'll find that love is what remains. When you celebrate, they celebrate with you – they live through your eyes and life experiences. The more joy and glory you insist upon for yourself, the more joy and glory you insist upon for them. Know that their love burns strongly for you at all times, regardless of whether you visit their resting place or stay at home. Do whatever rituals you need to do for yourself: set an extra place at the dinner table during the holidays; light a candle of remembrance on special occasions; make donations and take bold actions in their honour. Go where the love is and stay away from the bickering – people are speaking and acting from their pain, it's not who they really are. Love the babies in the family – they are life – and know that just as they are born into our world, Spirit celebrates as our loved ones who pass are born into theirs. Don't go back to work too early or stay away too long. Be honest, kind and patient with yourself. And then, one plain Wednesday, as you're going about your day, it'll happen: you'll hear the whisper; you'll feel their presence; you'll smell their perfume; they'll come to you in a dream. And you'll know, when you're ready to know, that the pain is over and that love remains.

☆ Activation 1 ☆
The Power of Pain

Sometimes we suppress our grief. Perhaps we were brought up to believe it's wrong to cry or express our emotions, or maybe we were punished for doing so. Sometimes it's because we're afraid that if we grieve, our lives will end and we'll never see the light of day again, so we just don't go there. And sometimes our subconscious minds are not ready to let the person or animal go, and so deny us the reality of the transition in an effort to protect us.

Not experiencing the pain of grief seems like a good thing in the short term, but unexpressed grief can lead to all kinds of pain and problems later on. You wouldn't leave a broken bone untreated, so why do so with a broken heart?

The grief of bereavement hurts a lot for many of us, and so the temptation to run away from it, stifle it, shove it down or deny it is great. But we have these feelings for a reason, and expressing them allows us to get the pain out of our systems, to go on to live meaningful lives and experience profound relationships with our loved ones in Spirit in a new way.

By permitting ourselves to simply sit with the pain, become aware of it, observe it, we can begin the healing process. That's all I want you to do for this exercise. The next time you feel the pain of grief welling up, don't run away; don't quickly change the subject and think of something else. Instead, just close your eyes, put one hand on your heart and the other on your tummy and feel compassion for yourself. And allow yourself to observe the feeling of grief:

- Where in your body is the pain?

- What is the sensation like?

- Which emotions are there?

- What thoughts come to mind?

Let the series of emotions run their course and express themselves naturally. Observe them without judgement, and let them be without fear. Most emotions come in waves, so when the worst of the pain has subsided, thank it for its presence and for reminding you how much you loved the person or animal who passed away.

☆ Activation 2 ☆
Love Notes

When my gran passed away, part of my pain was due to unanswered questions and untold truths. There were so many things I wanted to share with her, which played on repeat in my mind, getting stuck in my throat, remaining unexpressed. Then, out of sheer frustration and a need to get these things 'off my chest', I put pen to paper one day and wrote a letter to her. I scribbled for a whole hour and, afterwards, I felt a lot better. Strangely, not only did I feel that I'd got it off my chest, I also felt as though I'd expressed it to her, when I thought I'd missed my chance, and this really helped me to heal.

When you feel ready, find some quiet time to write to your loved one in Spirit. I'd like you to write two letters: one that focuses on the happy times, the good memories and your loving feelings; and another focusing on your anger, pain, disappointment, frustrations and unanswered questions.

Start with whichever one comes easiest. The aim of this exercise is for you to express your feelings fully: both the light side and the shadow side of your relationship with your loved one.

There is no right or wrong way to complete this exercise. My only guidance to you would be: don't hold back. If you ever felt that you couldn't tell your loved one how much you cared for them, or if you ever felt you couldn't tell them how much they hurt you (or, conversely, how sorry you are that you hurt them), well, now's your chance.

When you're done, make a conscious decision about what to do with your two letters. Is there one you want to keep and one you'd rather release? Do you want to share them with your support group, counsellor or therapist? Would you like to destroy them to aid your healing? Or do you wish to hang on to them a while longer? Do whatever feels right to you.

Now, onwards, to Chapter 2, which invites you to explore whether a loved one in Spirit has been trying to show you a sign. But first, a quick overview of what we've learned in Chapter 1.

CHAPTER HIGHLIGHTS

★ There is no right or wrong way to grieve. Let your feelings be what they are. Take your time.

★ You don't have to maintain a painful vigil to show your passed loved ones you care. It is in releasing yourself from this pain that you feel close to them again.

★ Expressing yourself in letters to your loved one can promote healing and feelings of relief and peace.

CHAPTER 2

FEELING THE SIGNS

This chapter will look at the personal, intimate experience of receiving a sign from Spirit. There are some encounters with Spirit that don't come via a medium, but seem like strange synchronicities: surprising moments of comfort; a feeling of presence. These moments are important because they give you a direct experience of Spirit that's often accompanied by a feeling of amazement, and they have a significant role to play in our exploration of mediumship because they lack a medium. What I mean by this is that if you receive a special sign from Spirit, and it's not through a medium, then it removes all doubt as to where the information came from. These moments can be small and they can be silly, but you'll know you had one because, no matter what anyone says or how many people don't 'get it', you won't be able to shake that feeling that it came from Spirit.

Ultimately, the only way we can really know Spirit is first-hand. I am aware that when I do my demonstrations, regardless of how amazing the communication may be, there's always that gap – the gap created by the need for the medium to relay the message from Spirit. When we receive a sign from Spirit directly, however, there is no such gap. This is why I've spent the last five years coaching and developing mediums, from complete beginners to advanced practitioners, so that more people are empowered to have profound first-hand experiences of Spirit.

It's very likely that you've had some kind of communication from your loved ones who've passed. Your own body is the very best instrument for detecting when a 'coincidence' is something more. And when you experience it first-hand, however small, there can be no room for doubt. You just feel it. You just know.

I've experienced signs in my personal life, some of which are shared here. Just the other day I was eating in a Japanese restaurant. There was a television at one end of the room, and I was facing away from it because it was showing the news and that bothers me. My fiancé was sitting opposite the TV, and mid-conversation he said, 'Aww, look!' about a news segment on baby turtles. Just as I turned around I saw on the subtitles that they'd called one of the turtles Albie – the name of my uncle who'd passed away and whom I love dearly. I got that little leap of butterflies in my tummy, and I knew it was a sign from him.

This, and other signs I've received, felt intentional, and I'd encourage you to look out for them in your own life too.

The signs our loved ones in Spirit leave us are many, but they each have one thing in common: they result in the uplifting and distinct feeling that they are from 'them'. I liken this to that feeling of receiving unexpected gifts when you were a child, or when you wake up in the morning and realize it's a special day. If you have received a sign and felt the loving presence of your family and friends in Spirit, cherish it and focus on that feeling of comfort and being uplifted. Give thanks and think of it often.

Some common signs that Spirit give us are as follows:

- Finding small coins

- Finding feathers

- Hearing a song that reminds you of a loved one

- Smelling a fragrance that you associate with them

- Dreaming of your loved ones

- Hearing someone call your/their name

- Looking up at the stars and feeling a presence, like someone is looking back

- A thought about your loved one suddenly popping into your mind

- Being given an item of theirs

- Being given a piece of jewellery that belonged to them

- Being given a symbol of faith that belonged to a loved one who passed, such as their prayer beads, a Saint Christopher coin or their Divination tools

But it can definitely get much weirder than these. Our loved ones in Spirit have a sense of humour and they'll try to reach us any way they can. My friend saw the face of her mum in Spirit in the foam of her cappuccino, and I myself received a strange sign from a loved one that I'd like to share with you now:

I sat up on a stool at the deli counter in my local high-end food market. I took a sip of Prosecco and reapplied my lipstick as I waited for my mum. I smoothed down my crisp, white shirt, and puffed up my skirt which was bright pink, to match my lipstick. My favourite teal wool coat was draped over the back of my stool and my feet were bedecked in a pair of bright orange Manolo Blahnik shoes. Mum and I were celebrating because I'd just stepped out of my final exam at university.

Mum sent me a text to say she was running late, so I got chatting with the woman behind the counter who had very kindly served me my Prosecco and a Mediterranean platter.

'I'll take a tea for my mum as well, please – we're celebrating, but she's driving.'

'Oh, lovely – what are you celebrating?'

'I sat my final exam at university today,' I beamed.

'Congratulations!' she said. 'My daughter is in her third year.'

And so the conversation went on. Then Mum arrived and we hugged.

'Congratulations!' Mum said. 'Your Grandpa Dale would be so proud of you.'

Grandpa Dale, my mum's father, had always encouraged me to stick it out at school and had always wanted me to go to university, but sadly he passed to Spirit when I was 13 – 11 years before I would set foot in my beloved University of Glasgow.

'That's odd,' our server said, whilst squinting at the till screen. 'A bottle of champagne has just appeared on your order. Did someone come and use this till?' she asked us, confused.

No one had, and Mum and I just smiled at each other, knowing that Grandpa Dale was getting a message to us that he was indeed proud of everything I'd achieved during my six years as a student of English Literature and Philosophy.

Whilst I believe that our loved ones in Spirit will always try to get a sign to us, especially on special occasions, or when we truly require it for our healing, there are some people who feel as if they have never had a sign, even though they were extremely close to the person who passed when they were living.

I'm afraid I don't know why some people receive lots of signs from Spirit and others don't. Over the years, however, I've noticed a few similarities between cases of people who haven't received signs, so if you're awaiting that comfort and evidence from your loved one, I hope this information will serve to increase the chances that you'll receive the miracle you seek.

You Got a Sign But You Missed It

I have no idea how often our loved ones in Spirit try to give us a sign, but I do know that there have been times in my life when it's seemed the signs were everywhere!

There are other times, however, when I've gone for months without feeling the presence of any of my loved ones at all, receiving not a peep of communication. I'm sure during these times, they are trying to give me signs, but I've missed them. This can happen for all sorts of reasons – being massively preoccupied with something else, being in a season of life that requires a more 'practical' energy, loss of faith or a drastic change in our environment... any or all of these can cause us to miss the signs our loved ones give us.

You Got a Sign But It Was Misaligned with Your Expectations

What would a 'sign' from your loved ones look like to you? Whenever my clients talk to me about having never received a sign, this is the first thing I ask them and mostly, they can't answer. Your loved one may have been trying to communicate with you, but you didn't know what to look out for. Or you may have had an expectation that's either very difficult for them to meet (like full materialization in front of you, on demand) or you are looking for one specific thing, whilst they are trying to show you another. You cannot be rigid in your expectations – you must allow your loved ones to do what they can on their own terms and be open to receiving it.

Your Need Is Too Great

It is a brutal and mysterious irony that if you're still suffering deeply from a loss, or if you are in the depths of depression, you will probably not get a sign from your loved ones in Spirit. In my experience, this is because, although it's sad that they've died, signs from Spirit are miracles, and so they happen on the vibration of love and not sadness. If you are on the vibration of deep and bitter grief, it's just not possible for them to get a message to you – it's like trying to hear an opera 20 feet under the ocean.

You Haven't Accepted the Transition

If you haven't yet received a sign from a loved one, it may be because you haven't fully accepted the loss of their physical body and presence in your life. This is a process, and you have to give yourself the time you need to grieve. If you are afraid to let go, then you have not accepted them as Spirit. This, in turn, means they cannot communicate with you as Spirit because they need your participation as the recipient of their signs. When you have fully healed and accepted the possibility of having a new kind of relationship with your loved one who has passed, the signs will most probably begin for you.

You're Fearful

If you're really stressed, angry or chronically sad about something in your life, you may not receive a sign from your loved one because you are in the energy of fear. Whatever is causing difficult feelings needs to be resolved – not just so you can get a sign, but so you can have a better quality of life.

What needs to change for you to experience more loving emotions, more frequently? Start small, and as you make changes towards love, you give power to Spirit and may notice more signs.

You're Being Too Demanding

Looking too hard for a sign from your loved ones and feeling angry or frustrated when you don't get it, then becoming even more demanding and angry as a result is a vicious cycle. This cycle gains momentum because you are searching for resolution to your pain. Try instead to relax, forget all about it, go on with your life and allow the sign to come when you least expect it.

No Evidence Is Good Enough

If you're really honest with yourself, you may realize that you *have* had a sign – or many signs – but that they haven't taken the pain away, convinced you or comforted you in the way you'd hoped, and so you've dismissed them. Express gratitude to Spirit for anything you think may be a sign. Train yourself to see the miracle of their communication, rather than dismissing them. Although many people do get comfort from signs from their loved ones, healing is a collaborative process and you have to be ready and willing to be healed and comforted. If you feel frustrated that the signs you've received are 'not good enough', then you are holding yourself away from the healing. Release this way of thinking about signs and adopt an attitude of awareness and openness instead.

You're a Medium Yourself

Again, the irony here is not lost on me, but some mediums rarely, if ever, receive signs from their own loved ones in Spirit. This is because they don't need them; they already know that their loved ones still exist, by virtue of the fact that they are able to give such evidence to others.

☆ ☆ ☆ ☆

If you have enough faith, and you have accepted that your loved one has made a transition into another way of being, it is very likely that, at some point in your life, you will have an experience that feels like they have given you a sign. Trust this feeling. But if all else fails in your attempts to receive a sign from a loved one, then you may take the initiative and go to them…

☆ ACTIVATION 3 ☆
Meeting Spirit Meditation

When your mind is calm and quiet, it acts as a bridge between our world and the world of Spirit. In meditation, anyone and everyone has access to their loved ones in Spirit (yes, even you!) and each of us can experience the comfort, reassurance and wisdom they have to offer us when we meet them in the space between worlds.

You will get better at meditation with practice. It can be challenging when your mind wants to jump all over the place and misbehave, but this is one meditation worth persevering with, because once you master it, you will experience personal and intimate confirmation beyond all other that your loved ones in Spirit are safe and well, and that you can 'pop next door' to be with them whenever you choose.

A word of advice before we begin: some people find it easy to visualize, others find listening easier; some people feel more during meditation and others smell, touch and taste the environment more easily. There is no right or wrong way, and the more you practise, the more you will discover what your dominant sense is in meditation. (Helpful hint: this will probably be your most dominant sense in your mediumship too.)

I am a visual person (predominantly clairvoyant and clairsentient), so I'm going to lead you through this experience as a visualization, but if you find it hard, feel free to focus on what you can hear, smell, touch, feel or taste instead – or, indeed, any other impressions that come to you.

You can also download the audio version of this meditation from my website – my gift to you: www.laurenrobertson.co.uk/mim/meditation1.

If you're ready to begin, make sure you're wearing comfortable clothing and you're sitting or lying down somewhere where you can be undisturbed for 30 minutes.

- Close your eyes, feel your body relaxing and take a few deep and nourishing breaths, feeling the oxygen expanding through your body, causing your muscles and tensions to relax even further.

- Take another deep breath and feel a final wave of relaxation lap over you.

- Bring your attention to the area a few inches in front of your mind's eye: you're standing in front of a heavy wooden door. Look at it, touch it, smell it. Get a sense of the environment as it seems to you. There are several shafts of light coming from behind the door – whatever's out there must be very bright. With ease, you unlatch the door and push it open, and your awareness is drenched in the most beautiful warm and healing light. As your eyes adjust to the light, you're met with the most glorious sight... a lush, green garden – paradise.

- Take one step forwards, out of the darkness and into the light.

- What can you see? What can you smell? What do you hear? What can you taste? What can you feel on your skin? Which emotions do you feel? Pay attention to your senses as you stand here in paradise.

- You begin to move down the path set out before you, and as you do, the beauty and glory of this place grows and grows, filling you with inspiration, excitement, love and security.

- As you move and the wondrous sensations grow stronger, you reach an opening. The narrow path expands into a wide circle, surrounded by nature, light and your favourite animals and plants. At the centre of the circle there is a bench – there's no one sitting there just yet. Go and take your place on the bench. You're here to meet someone and they'll be arriving shortly. Take a deep breath in and out, and enjoy being at peace in this environment.

- Shortly, you hear soft footsteps coming from behind a high wall and garden gate. As the gate clicks open, you are astonished and delighted to see a most beloved person who's made the journey from the Spirit World to be with you here. Look how young, happy, glowing and radiant they are! Your beloved embraces you in a long and meaningful hug, as they take their place on the bench with you – each of you eager to catch up with how the other is doing. Your loved one's eyes are so filled with wisdom and compassion – they've seen a thing or two since returning home to Spirit. They've gained a much higher perspective on life.

- This is your chance to tell them what you always wanted them to know. This is your opportunity to ask for their advice. Now is your chance to ask your question and have it answered. This is your opportunity to receive their perspective.

- Take some time to converse with your loved one – pay attention to how you feel and to your senses. Speak to them, laugh with them and confide in them your truth. This is your time to receive love and guidance, and your beloved is only too happy to oblige.

- As your conversation draws to a close, pay attention to how you feel – being emotional, elated, a lightness of being and clarity are normal.

- As your beloved rises to leave, you embrace once more, and as you watch them depart through the gate, they turn for one last wave and smile. And you know, as they vanish from sight, that they can never disappear from mind, or Spirit, and you know that this is your space together, and you can return here any time to be with them.

- Take in the glorious paradise one last time, and begin now, to make your way back through the foliage, up the path and towards the heavy door. And as you step from the light into the shade, you carry the feeling and essence of your loved one with you.

- As the shade gathers around you, you begin to feel 'within' your body once more. You begin to feel the surface underneath you, and the sounds of the room and your environment return.

- When you feel you have returned, wiggle your fingers, wiggle your toes and, when you're ready, open your eyes.

- Make some notes in your journal about your experience, your feelings and the wisdom you received. Set a date for the next time you'll return to meet your loved one in paradise.

CHAPTER HIGHLIGHTS

★   You will know a sign from Spirit by how it makes you feel.

★   Pay attention to your body – do you feel goosebumps, a sudden feeling of elation and love, butterflies in your tummy, a sense of 'knowing', an awareness of a presence? These are the best indicators of a sincere sign from Spirit.

★   There are many possible reasons you haven't received a sign from Spirit. Most of them can be addressed and simply require you to be in a different state of mind.

CHAPTER 3

DREAMIUMSHIP

There's one sign commonly received from loved ones in Spirit that I rank above all others because, in my experience, it happens to those of us with a strong, natural potential for mediumship.

One night, a few months after my gran passed away, I had the most unbelievably vivid dream. I dreamed I was in her house, sitting in the living room. The house was in silence and sunlight was streaming in through the window, shedding golden rays across the room and onto the carpet. *Why am I here?* I thought. *Gran died, I shouldn't be here.*

Suddenly, I heard the familiar sound of tea mugs, a sugar bowl, a milk jug and a plate of biscuits being placed on an embossed metal tray. It was coming from the serving hatch between the kitchen and living room. I knew that sound, and I knew it well – it was the sound of my childhood, the sound of my gran.

It can't be… I thought. I knew I was dreaming, and I knew she'd died. And yet the living room door swung open and there she stood, holding that metal tray.

'Have you eaten?' she asked, beaming.

She looked divine: youthful, happy, free, perfect, beautiful, peaceful, strong. Gone was the moth wing, and in its place stood my beautiful gran.

'You can't be here,' I said, ever the obstinate teenager. 'You died.'

'Well, I am here,' she replied, radiant.

I questioned, 'How do I know it's really you? How do I know I'm not just making all this up?'

Smiling, with love in her happy blue eyes, she placed the tray down on the coffee table, stood toe-to-toe with me, placed both index fingers lightly on my hips, and all 5 feet 2 inches of her lifted all 5 feet 8 inches of me gently off the ground, as if I were weightless.

'Whenever you dream of me, it's really me,' she told me. 'And when other people dream of their loved ones who've made the crossing, it's really them too. It's going to be your job to tell people this.'

My feet grazed the floor and I woke up. I didn't realize it at the time, but in retrospect, this was my first experience as a medium.

Paying Visits

If you dream about your loved ones in Spirit, this indicates you have abilities as a medium. I believe this because with all other signs, Spirit has to come the whole way into our world, giving us tangible, physical signs that they are around. But when we dream of our loved ones in Spirit, we are stepping halfway into theirs. I often tell my audience that a dream of a loved one in Spirit is a visitation – what I don't usually mention is that it's we who are visiting them. When you dream of your loved ones in Spirit and the dream seems real, clear, tangible, uplifting and healing, cherish it, because you have experienced 'dreamiumship'.

In a study conducted on mediums, aimed at examining their brain states when they are receiving communication from a Spirit person, one of the results was that the production of alpha brainwaves correlates with accuracy. The researchers came to this conclusion by measuring the brainwaves of several mediums as they answered questions about a person in Spirit whom they did not know, and had never met. Their answers were then given to a living person who knew the person in Spirit, who anonymously checked the medium's answers for accuracy. The wave activity of the medium's brain was observed using EEG, and, at the time the medium was giving information marked 'accurate' by the volunteer recipient; this coincided with raised levels of alpha brainwaves in the medium's brain.

You may think, then, that alpha brainwaves are reserved only for mediums, but actually, we all have them. Alpha brainwaves are correlated with a feeling of wakeful relaxed-alertness. What is strange about alpha brainwaves is that, for many of us, they also occur for a short time whilst we are sleeping. Why this happens is unknown. If you are producing alpha brainwaves during sleep, you're spontaneously entering the very same brain state associated with accurate mediumship.

So it's my belief that we each have some ability to communicate with our loved ones in Spirit.

☆ Activation 4 ☆
Sleep, Perchance to Dream

If you want to dream about your loved ones in Spirit, all you have to do is ask, and prepare yourself to receive. I cannot, of course, guarantee that you will meet your loved one in your dream; I can only share with you what has worked for me.

Since that initial experience with my gran, I have often dreamed of my loved ones in Spirit, and have conversed with them and received wisdom, insight and, occasionally, even predictions and premonitions. There were two instances in which my loved ones came to me in dreams that were particularly vivid and significant, and they had two things in common: first, I had a specific need/question that I wanted their help with; and second, I deliberately set the intention that I would meet my loved one in my dream. And so in this exercise, I invite you to do the same.

Step 1: why do you want to meet your loved one? What do you need help with? What question do you have for them? Get clear on the purpose of your meeting. Write out your question in your journal or on a piece of paper to clarify and crystallize your intention.

Step 2: create a bedtime ritual that will encourage sleep, restfulness and relaxation. You could perhaps take an aromatherapy bath, purchase some lovely new jammies, go to bed early or have a relaxing herbal drink before bed. Definitely make sure the room is tidy, as dark as possible and all technology (especially blue-lit screens) are switched off an hour before bed. You may also want to keep your journal and a pen beside your bed, in case you want to write down any guidance/inspiration received in your dream as soon as you wake up.

Step 3: get comfy in bed as you normally would and take a few deep and nourishing breaths. Breathe in for a slow count of three, hold for three, then breathe out for a slow count of three. Repeat until you feel nice and relaxed.

Step 4: visualize, or say in your mind what your intention is for your dream. Call out to your loved one in your mind and ask them to be with you. Set the intention that you will dream of your loved one in Spirit, that they will be happy to impart to you the answer to your question and provide the guidance you seek.

Step 5: drift off and dream sweetly.

Step 6: when you awake you may want to write down your experiences and any insights that came to you during the night. Even if you did not have a clear and fulfilling meeting with your loved one, or if your dream was cryptic, I'd still recommend writing it down and making some notes about your experience. The mind works in mysterious ways and even the most cryptic dreams can hold the answers you seek.

For me, intentional, focused dreaming feels like a workout for the mind, and most nights, I prefer to allow my mind to rest during sleep. For this reason, I attempt this mode of communication no more than once a week.

CHAPTER HIGHLIGHTS

★ Our brains produce alpha brainwaves, both when we are participating in mediumship and when we are asleep.

★ Dreaming of a loved one in Spirit may be thought of as a 'visitation' in which your loved one can impart guidance, comfort, wisdom and confirmation of their continued existence to you.

★ Dreamiumship is often indicative of mediumistic abilities.

CHAPTER 4

GIFTED VS LEARNED

I didn't see Spirit as a child. There were no people standing at the foot of my bed, nor did I glimpse anyone drifting down corridors. Never did I see transparent people following solid ones as they went about their lives…

The first time I realized I was a medium, I was giving a psychic/angel card reading to a woman in the freezing basement of a dingy Glasgow pub. We were both perched on upturned beer crates and I was reading her cards atop a barrel that had been turned into a table with the help of a piece of MDF scavenged from deeper in the cellar.

Whilst my friends from school were flipping burgers, I was flipping cards: beautiful, magical cards that allowed me to see into my recipients' lives – their past pains and pleasures, their current concerns and things they were likely to encounter in the future. And I loved it.

I loved the look on my clients' faces when they finally understood that the universe was watching them with kind eyes, because I'd uttered something so true I could not have guessed it. I could spend hours talking and listening, about the things that were important to them. It was an honour to look intimately at who, and what, my clients spent their days thinking about, longing for, pining after. And I loved travelling with them, through their innermost thoughts and feelings, both as a guest and as a guide. It was a privilege to be the one to let them know they weren't alone – that somebody, somewhere, saw the truth, without judgement, and cared about them and their lives.

In this particular pub, on this particular day, the deepest, innermost pain of my recipient was about to come bubbling to the surface of her reading, changing both our lives for ever.

I had led her on a whistle-stop tour of her own life via the angel cards, and we had come to the Archangel Raziel – angel of wisdom, learning, discovery and intelligence, who is often depicted looking like Gandalf with a penchant for gold garments. I had just let my gaze fall upon the card and begun to speak of its meaning, when the most peculiar feeling crept over me.

It was a cool warmth, a prickly comfort, a creeping feeling of love – a presence, although no one was there. It began in the space behind my left shoulder, making its way along my arm, down my back and then up, through my neck and head, giving me the strangest sensation that I can only describe as *activation*.

I looked up at her, with the intention of enquiring whether she could feel it too, but as soon as I lifted my head something was revealed to me. In that split second it became clear to me why she had come for this reading, what the source of her pain was and who she wanted to talk about... because he was standing right beside me. Not in a Swayze-in-*Ghost* kinda way, but in my mind, in my awareness, in my feelings and in my heart.

'I need to talk about your dad,' I said, tentatively. Her head shot up and I could see her eyes becoming glassy with tears.

This was all new territory to me, and what with the emotion on her face, the feeling making its way into my head and the presence of the man standing inside my mind, I don't mind telling you I was quietly terrified.

'Has your dad passed away?' I asked her outright.

'Yes,' she replied.

'I hope you don't mind me saying this, but your dad is here. Is it OK with you if I describe him and you can tell me if you want me to stop?' I asked, my heart racing.

'Yes,' she sobbed.

I described to her all that I was seeing and feeling that felt foreign. It was as if they weren't my own thoughts – as if someone had planted them and the only way to get them out was to explain them. I told her that I saw a tall man with rosy cheeks, overweight and loving, with a great sense of humour and a couple of teeth missing at the back, with gaps you could see when he laughed. I saw him wearing a shirt and jeans, and could tell that he cared very much for his daughter. I saw his bad habits. I saw his refusal to change. I saw the heart attack. I felt the pain of having been denied a final farewell to those he loved so much.

Tears were pouring down her face at this point and, as I gazed at her, I saw the burden of guilt expressing itself in her eyes. Her face was bright red and she was wiping her tears furiously with a smushed-up old tissue, making it redder still.

'What's his name? Can you tell me his name?' she blurted out.

My heart raced faster and my palms began to sweat as in a second I was tossed into the eternal, internal struggle of all mediums: on one hand, the belief that uttering the name of a deceased person whom you have never met, under such circumstances, and having this person acknowledge it as correct, was just not possible; and on the other hand, the absolutely still, calm, powerful certainty that somehow we are all connected, and that everything is possible – miracles are real and this man's name, like all other truths, is right on the tip of your tongue… all you have to do is say it.

Suddenly, a name cut through the internal confusion. I doubted it because it was one that was already familiar to me, but I so badly wanted to please her and her father, and it was all I had.

'There's only one name coming to me,' I said, apologetically. 'And it's a name that's familiar to me, so my mind might be making it up…' I warned. 'But I'm going to say it anyway. The only name that's coming to my mind is James… Jim.'

She looked at me and I couldn't tell whether her face was painted with disappointment or amazement.

'Oh God – that was his name. It's really my dad!'

The tears flowed and, as I gave her space to cry it out, I felt utterly overwhelmed with joy and gratitude, expansiveness and confusion – like being rescued from a sinking boat in the cold black sea. I felt that somehow, I'd been allowed to be a part of someone else's true love. It was the feeling of a miracle.

As the reading came to a close, she got up and embraced me in a bear hug. And there we stood, two souls, hugging, surrounded by beer crates, popping funnels and barrels, in the freezing basement of a pub.

When I got home that night, I locked myself in my room and hid under the duvet, like Spider-Man when he discovers his powers for the first time and worries that he's a danger to humanity.

What Is Mediumship?

Mediumship, at its core, is the practice of attempting to prove the existence of life after bodily death. The kind that I practise is called mental mediumship, meaning that all communication comes through me, as the person in Spirit impresses true information about themselves into my mind. I then convey this information to a recipient – usually a loved one who knew the communicator well, and he or she confirms whether or not the information is accurate. If enough of the information given is accurate, and they are confident beyond reasonable doubt that it was not obtained from elsewhere, then this proves the existence of another intelligence. This is the continued intelligence of the person in Spirit.

Now, in the age of technology, we are being given the language with which to talk about mediumship and Spirit communication. Human beings have become experts at building disembodied intelligence, information and interaction. Think of social media: when your computer goes offline, when it's switched off, all your photos, posts, videos, shared experiences, likes, dislikes, frustrations and happy memories remain. To me, this is a perfect analogy for what happens when we die: our bodies go offline, but the bits that made us *feel*, that signified who we were and what we cared about, remains. So just as we can log into social media from a different computer, I maintain that we can 'log in' to people's memories and feelings from a different body. With mediumship the medium is given access to the 'memory and feeling' account of the person in Spirit.

The True Purpose of Mediumship

The point of mediumship is not whether or not God exists. It's not to give cold, hard evidence that satisfies the sceptics. Mediumship is in service to humanity – its function is to help us remember and create love, connection and healing in our lives. It serves to give joy to those whose lives have been stolen by grief, and freedom to those whose lives have been starved by the fear of death in all its forms.

True spirit communication – the kind where everyone in the room is in floods of tears and the person receiving the message feels that his or her loved one is present without a shadow of a doubt – has the power to heal two of the worst experiences of being human: the fear of death and the pain of loss.

When we are no longer afraid of death, and we are able to heal the painful feelings that come from believing we've said goodbye for ever to our loved ones, our entire lives can go through a miraculous transformation. We can go from depression, grief, insomnia, sickness, fear, loneliness, anger and hopelessness to love, abundance, health, fulfilment, forgiveness, openness, generosity and optimism. When we are free of the fear of death and the pain of loss, we can rekindle a zest for life and achieve love, friendships, strong family relationships, good health, wealth, emotional freedom and other miracles. When we receive communication from a loved one in Spirit, we see that there is nothing to fear – we cannot possibly die – and that our beloveds have not ceased to exist either.

I have been privileged to receive, to witness and to be a part of such transformations as a result of mediumship. There is one instance that sticks out in my mind of when I was demonstrating mediumship at a local spiritualist church. A young woman was sitting alone on my far left and, as my gaze connected with hers, the name Joanne was whispered into my ear. So I told her straight, 'I have a message for you, and it's simply the name Joanne.' The woman's metamorphosis, before my very eyes, was astounding. I watched her change from someone who looked as if their blood ran cold with sadness, to someone who'd had an instant transfusion of sunshine. Her face went from bitter to elated in a second.

'Joanne is my daughter who died,' she said, 'and every day I come here and I ask her silently, in my mind, in prayer, for her name, just her name. And today I got it. I know it was her.'

I have seen this woman several times since and she looks like someone who discovered the fountain of youth – glowing, young, free and radiant. That, dear reader, is the point of mediumship.

So, you might ask, if that's the point of mediumship, who gets to be a part of something so wonderful – what does it take to be a medium?

The Anatomy of a Medium

Who is a medium? What does a medium look like? What are the qualities of a medium?

The qualities of an excellent medium might surprise you. In my experience, they are no different from those of an amazing musician, a talented painter, a masterful brain surgeon or a successful and wealthy entrepreneur. Becoming a great medium is less about being born with a mysterious and yet immediately clear and flawless 'gift' of Spirit communication, and more about whether you are willing to do what it takes to make the very best of what you've got. For me, there was a burning desire to know people intimately, to help them by listening and talking and to empower them by allowing them to feel loved and deeply understood. This desire only grows stronger by the day, and has given me urgency to be the best medium I can be. I am by no means the best medium there is, but you'd have difficulty finding one who cares more about the souls she serves.

You too must find some kind of desire like this within yourself. You must be clear about what drives you. You must instil within yourself the belief that you *can* and *will* succeed. And you must decide that you are truly prepared to do whatever is necessary to become a Spirit communicator through whom miracles are possible. It is often said about psychic work, and especially mediumship, that extraordinary claims require extraordinary evidence, and so to become a great medium requires the commitment to becoming extraordinary. Your commitment to your journey – both your personal growth and your studies as a medium – is of much greater value than natural talent without the mindset and dedication. If you have both, then you are blessed.

Yes, there are people who are born with an exceptional ability to connect with Spirit, just as there are those who are born with an extraordinary ability to play the piano. But there are also many excellent musicians who had seemingly little 'natural' ability, yet plenty of desire and faith… and I think the same is true of many great mediums.

All the world-class mediums I know of have the qualities outlined below to a greater or lesser degree. And a unique combination of these is what makes them so good at conveying the manner and essence of Spirit in their own special way. I have yet to come across a mental medium who has any additional magical power over and above these qualities. What *is* magical, however, is the medium's dedication to becoming self-aware, building on their strengths and committing to their mediumship practice as a lifestyle.

Desire

For me, this is the element upon which all other aspects of being a successful medium depend. A strong and sincere desire to work with Spirit and to be of service to people is essential. The journey to developing mediumship can be challenging, and when situations arise that cause you to doubt, make you want to turn back or shatter any expectations you had, this desire is the only thing that will keep you going. There have been numerous times when I've wanted to quit. From a run of weak connections and abuse on social media, to doubting my abilities because I couldn't give my recipient what they wanted – the reasons are many, but what's always got me back on the platform, turning up for the next reading, doing a meditation even when I don't feel like it, is knowing that I can be a vessel for love and comfort for someone who might really need it. And as long as that's in any way true, I just can't stay away.

Faith

From what I have experienced, and what I've seen from other mediums, the more faith you have in yourself and Spirit, the better your mediumship will be. I used to say I have total faith in Spirit, I just don't trust myself, until the download came one day that saying this was weakening my mediumship. I am Spirit, and you are Spirit, so you cannot trust Spirit and not trust yourself. You cannot be a great medium if you don't trust yourself or have faith in yourself. This is the journey of the medium, and this is why the course of becoming a great medium is inextricably linked to that of self-mastery – of becoming a more confident, self-aware and peaceful person. The more you are able to trust yourself, trust the process and trust Spirit, the more you make yourself available for the communication to happen. In an age when we are being invited to doubt ourselves, our worth, our value and our abilities, daily, in myriad forms, maintaining self-belief can be a lifelong commitment.

Resilience

You must develop the ability to bounce back. When you get a series of 'nos', when things are going awry in your personal life or you feel disappointed or let down, you have to be able to zoom out and see the bigger picture. The temptation can be to withdraw from spiritual practices when you're going through a hard time, in favour of dealing with more practical matters, but the best mediums I know have become more resilient through using their mediumship during difficult times. They actually thrive, learn, love and grow from challenges, and they seek solace in practising their mediumship, rather than shelving it until they feel better. If you can find a way to be of service to Spirit in even the worst of times, you will not only give much healing to others who are suffering, but you will also receive it as you do so. My boss who ran the psychic company I worked for in the early days made me go out to work the day my grandfather died, and it's the best thing she could've done for me. Being of service to people who had gone through what I was then experiencing gave me access to inner strength, greater compassion, deeper connections, a softness and openness to Spirit that helped all of us that night.

Commitment

Attending the odd workshop here and there isn't enough to achieve excellence in your mediumship – just like going to the occasional piano lesson isn't enough if you want to play in a world-class orchestra. If you want to excel at anything, you need to set up conditions that allow you to regularly practise, grow, learn and develop. When it comes to mediumship, this usually means a meditation practice that you do every day, plenty of study, training and gathering information and lots of opportunities to use your mediumship with all different kinds of personalities, both in Spirit and living. It also means a commitment to learning about yourself. If *you're* not growing, your gifts can't grow. You have to be dedicated to looking after yourself, and doing what you need to do to be in the best position to work with Spirit. Sometimes this can mean giving up thoughts, feelings or situations that no longer serve you, and sometimes it means adding to your life in the form of self-care, learning, new ideas, new behaviours, new people or new emotions.

Selflessness

To be a medium, you have to be 'selfless' in two distinct ways. First, you must indeed think of others before yourself at times. You must be prepared to give of yourself generously for the benefit of others. Sometimes the work of Spirit and the need of the recipient have to be more important than you. Second, you have to learn to literally lose your sense of 'self' when working to allow Spirit to impress information upon you.

Focus

There's a certain state of mind you need to be in to work as a medium – one that our waking lives do not usually require of us. As a rule, we need to be hyperstimulated mental multitaskers, often in a state of high anxiety. Mediumship, on the other hand, calls on us to transcend these frantic states. A spiritual practice, then, is usually necessary to teach your mind to move from its frantic state to that needed for mediumship. The receptive state in which mediumship takes place is usually cultivated over time and might include meditation, journaling, self-care rituals, yoga, tai chi, martial arts, walking your dog in the park or daily gratitude. The fun is in finding what works for you, and the point is to commit to training your mind to be in a receptive state of relaxed alertness.

Communication skills

Although the point of mental mediumship is that a person in Spirit speaks or acts through you, the fact is, it's still you who are doing the speaking, and your mind that must confidently make sense of the ideas. I'd go so far as to argue that in mental mediumship, people in Spirit cannot speak about anything that isn't already available in your consciousness. So the more you develop your vocabulary, the greater the expression you are able to make on behalf of Spirit. Also, there is a performance aspect to mediumship, whether you are in a one-to-one reading or on a platform, and again, it's up to you as the medium to deliver the information from Spirit in an appropriate way. There's nothing worse than a medium who gets great information, but bores the audience to tears, or even says something insensitive. Mediumship is a collaboration between yourself and Spirit. Spirit brings the information, but you must take responsibility for communicating it in the clearest, kindest, most compelling way possible.

Compassion

The idea that you need compassion to be a great medium is so obvious that I nearly didn't bother listing it here. But I decided to include it because I think it's worth restating that it's not just the recipient or the communicator in Spirit you need to have compassion for… you also need it for yourself. And it's not enough to be compassionate when you're up on that platform or in a one-to-one. If you want to be a great medium, compassion needs to be a way of life for you. Whatever makes you feel connected to other people fortifies your mediumship and, conversely, whatever disconnects you from them weakens it. Compassion – the attitude of understanding, accepting and being kind – is the most powerful connector of all.

Desire to Learn

Mediumship is a process in which you never stop learning – you can always be better, more loving, more compassionate, more consistent, more compelling, more polished. You yourself, as a medium, are a deep well with as yet unknown ways of connecting with Spirit. To be a *great* medium, you have to be willing to dive deep into new approaches and uncover areas within yourself that need to be loved, accepted or healed. The process of learning is never-ending.

Desire to Do Better

Great mediums are always prepared to do better: to look at how strong the connection to Spirit was, how clearly the message came through and how strong the evidence was – all in a critical, but not self-critical way. They evaluate so they can do better next time.

You must learn not to be ashamed of the things you get wrong because there will be many. The desire to always do better requires you to examine and explore why a certain message went well, whilst another went badly, and adjust your approach accordingly. Being embarrassed, ashamed, shy or paralysed by doubt for long periods of time only serves to prolong the lesson that needs to be learned. Lean into it and explore it, but don't take it personally, and your mediumship will improve as a result.

Sense of Humour

This might seem like an odd prerequisite in the context of people who've died or who've lost loved ones, but from what

I'm told, there is no doom and gloom after death and people in Spirit don't want to be depressing or for their loved ones to be depressed; they tend to want to elevate and bring joy and laughter – especially if that was their nature in life. Loosen up and be open to this.

Joy

A miserable person makes a miserable medium. If you want to be a great medium, you need to make a point of being joyful in your life, whatever that means to you.

Love

In mediumship, love is everything. It is the bond that makes communication possible. It is the force that compels the communicator, the medium and the recipient to arrive at the same place at the same time so that communication can take place. And if you don't know love, then you don't know Spirit. Get to know what love means to you and cultivate it carefully, watering it often. The more familiar you are with love in your life, the more love there will be in your mediumship.

☆ ☆ ☆ ☆

How many of the above qualities do you recognise in yourself? The more you have, the better your potential to be a great medium. If you desire it enough, and are willing to develop the self-awareness to take stock of your progress in developing and enhancing these qualities, the more likely it is that you can be a medium – both in the sense that you can more closely connect with your own loved ones in Spirit and that you can help others connect with theirs.

I've created the following coaching questions and exercises to help you cultivate the qualities of a medium. Just as a piano tutor would assess the existing knowledge and experience of a new student, so we must be clear on where you are now in relation to the qualities outlined above and devise the most authentic and valuable way for you to move forwards with each of them. We must take stock of where you are in your development in order to create a strong and true foundation upon which to build. If you desire to be a medium who conveys the reality of the Spirit World in a way that truly helps people, you must first know and help yourself.

Answer the following questions in your journal. Be you. Be honest. Be thorough. There are no wrong answers. What matters is that your answers feel full and true for you.

☆ Activation 5 ☆
Unfolding Your Truth

Desire

- Why is it important to you that you develop your mediumship?

- What are the values you hold dear, based on the reasons you gave in the previous question? (For example, healing, contribution, respect, love, significance, transformation, etc.)

- Are there important reasons that you didn't write because you think they're 'unspiritual'? Write these down too. (For example, I want to be famous; I want to feel powerful; I want to matter; I want to have an impact; I want to travel the world; I want to be respected, etc.)

Faith

- Can you describe a time when you had absolute faith that you'd succeed?

- What (if anything) about working with Spirit causes you to lose faith in yourself or Spirit?

- What are the differences between the two examples you just wrote about? What needs to happen for your work with Spirit to take on the qualities of 'knowing that you will succeed'?

Resilience

- Describe a time when you bounced back from something difficult.

- What might prevent you from bouncing back to confidence in your mediumship?

- What's the next step you must take to become more resilient?

Commitment

- On a scale of 1–10 (where 1 is not at all committed and 10 is completely committed), how committed are you to developing your connection with Spirit? Why did you give this answer?

- What are you currently doing in your life to demonstrate this level of commitment?
- What are you doing that shows you're not committed to the extent you say you are?

Your Sense of Self

- What in life triggers/causes you to become self-conscious?
- Which aspects of mediumship cause you to become stuck in your own thinking?
- Make a list of occasions when you've been caught up in the action of life and lost your sense of self-consciousness. What, if anything, do they have in common?

Focus

- Which activities in life do you enjoy focusing on?
- How could you bring more activities like this into your life?
- What needs to happen to transfer this enjoyable focus onto your mediumship practice?

Communication Skills

- On a scale of 1–10 (where 1 is not at all and 10 is completely), how confident are you in communicating with others in a clear, compelling and compassionate way? Why did you give yourself that score? What would be a 10 for you?

- When you envision yourself doing mediumship at the peak of your capabilities, what are the qualities of the way you communicate? How do you want your mediumship to sound?

- What do you need to do to get closer to that ideal?

Compassion

- Towards whom are you lacking compassion? Make a list.

- What would compassion for these people look like to you?

- Choose one person from the list (you'll know who to pick by how it feels – trust yourself) and perform the act of compassion you just wrote.

Desire to Learn

- Take stock of your experiences with Spirit so far. How much mediumship training have you had? What was the nature of your training (books, lectures, workshops, mentorship, etc.)?

- What have you been unwilling to learn in mediumship to this point? Make a list. (For example, you may have been unwilling to learn to have confidence in yourself, how to see mistakes as a blessing or how to receive names, dates, etc.)

- Pick something you've been unwilling to learn until this point. How could you make it the focus of your learning? Create a plan to do so.

Desire to Do Better

- How do you feel/what thoughts do you have when you doubt yourself?

- How can you turn these into a constructive critique?

- Get into the habit of critiquing your mediumship objectively – without emotion and not taking it as a condemnation of your person.

Sense of Humour

- Make a list of five things that have made you laugh.

- What was funny about them? How does laughing make you feel?

- How might laughter serve you in your mediumship?

Joy

- When was the last time you felt pure joy?

- Close your eyes and turn the 'volume' up on that feeling – what thoughts come to mind?

- What needs to happen for you to experience more instances of joy in your life?

Love

- Who do you love? Who loves you?

- What are you doing/not doing that lets you know you're being unloving towards yourself?

- What does love mean to you?

By answering the questions above, you have unlocked new doors to your connection with Spirit. Your work with Spirit is a mirror of yourself, your beliefs, your emotions and your life experiences. That which you experience in life, you experience with Spirit. By bringing to consciousness the beliefs that you carry about yourself and the world, as they pertain to mediumship, you have demonstrated that you have what it takes to be a medium and that you already use it in your daily life.

Earlier in the chapter we asked who is a medium? It seems that we have found the answer. The answer is you.

Your strengths in your mediumship are a direct reflection of your strengths as a human being. Although a person in Spirit will bring you the information as clearly as they can, it's your job to receive, understand and pass it along in the clearest way possible.

This is where we see that mediumship is truly a collaboration between Spirit and self, and to make the very best of a message from Spirit, you have to make the very best of yourself. One of the main problems faced by new mediums is that they think they have to say and do what their tutor says and does, but if that's not your natural way of speaking and being, it will sound strange, disconnected and insincere. It's like trying on an outfit that looks great on your best friend but is just so not 'you'.

Great mediumship is a confident, spacious and honest blend of your awareness and the intelligence of the Spirit person. You don't have to be anyone but you to be a great medium, and to know and be the best version of yourself is to give the best tools to Spirit to use.

Earlier, I described qualities which are not directly involved with the transmission of information from Spirit per se, but which support your practice and raw talent and enable you to present evidence in as clear and confident a way as possible – like a diamond in a beautiful setting. I encourage you to develop these skills and have fun doing so. Sign up for toastmasters to develop your communication skills, take a counselling course and learn how to really listen, go out and meet new people from different backgrounds. Often, the skills that take a medium's work from good to great have nothing to do with their ability to receive the information, and are more to do with the medium having never developed the skills that support the delivery of the information. Take time to learn whatever skills tickle your fancy, trusting that they are Spirit-led. Doing so will help your mediumship to be the best it can be.

There is just one other area of strength I'd like to help you identify and develop that will be pertinent and relevant to your mediumship.

☆ Activation 6 ☆
Exploring Your Strengths – the Clairs

Take out your journal and a pen or something to type with or speak into, whichever you prefer.

Now, I want you to think of a happy memory – somewhere beautiful you've visited or a time in your life you think of fondly. Got it? Good.

Now, either by writing, typing or speaking, I want you to describe the memory in as much detail as possible. A few paragraphs will do nicely.

Done? Great! Now I want you to review what you've written/said and notice whether you've used mostly:

- seeing words

- hearing words

- feeling words

- scent words

- taste words

- thinking words.

Which have you predominantly used?

- If you have used seeing words, you are predominantly clairvoyant.

- If you have used hearing words, you are predominantly clairaudient.

- If you have used feeling words, you are mostly clairsentient.

- If you have used scent words, you are predominantly clairessent.

- If you have used taste words, you are predominantly clairgustant.

- If you have used thinking words, you are primarily claircognizant.

The 'clairs' are the different senses through which we receive information from Spirit in our mediumship, and your dominant 'clair' is usually a reflection of the sense you engage most with in life. You can tell which sense(s) will be central to your mediumship by the words you use to describe your memories and experiences.

Clairvoyance, clairaudience and clairsentience are the most common, with the others often playing a supporting role. Most great mediums have a holistic experience of Spirit, meaning that information comes through each and all of these channels at different times. In addition, we sometimes just have a strong gut feeling about what the communicator in Spirit is trying to tell us.

The more clearly you can identify your dominant 'clair' and develop it, the clearer and more concise the information you receive from Spirit will be. Remember – Spirit loves you and wants to work with your strengths, so it's your job to know what those are.

A great and simple way to develop your dominant 'clair' is to pay more deliberate and conscious attention to it in your daily life:

- How could you appreciate the visual beauty of your life more?

- How could you listen more carefully when others are speaking?

- When could you be more emotionally present, rather than absent-minded in your life?

- How could you enjoy tasting, smelling, feeling, thinking more?

Try 'turning up' your dominant clair for one week and discover what happens. Remember to write about it in your journal to track your progress.

CHAPTER HIGHLIGHTS

★ **The purpose of mediumship is to prove the existence of life after death, to help our recipients heal from the fear of death and the pain of loss.**

★ **You now know your dominant 'clair' – this is the primary means by which Spirit will communicate with you.**

★ **Excellence in mediumship arises from a combination of qualities, all of which are available to you!**

CHAPTER 5

WHAT'S LOVE GOT TO DO WITH IT?

I let my eyes and hands wander along the rail of multi-coloured dresses, allowing the hues and textures to speak to me. I was looking for something to wear. It was a special occasion – very early on in my mediumship journey – and I was going to be demonstrating at a spiritualist church for the first time.

Seeing nothing I liked, I left the store in Paisley, where I lived, and began to wander uphill towards the top of the high street. All day I'd been filled with feelings of anxiety, excitement, fear and love, in anticipation of the work I was to do in just a few short hours' time.

As I walked, the thoughts came faster and faster: *what if I mess up? What if no one in Spirit comes through? What if I don't feel anything? Is it inappropriate to wear stilettos to a spiritualist church? Is it really a church? Will there be hymns? What if I don't know them? What if I don't know anyone there? What if I do know someone there? Will I meet their expectations? I really want to do a great job. I don't want to do this. I can't do this. This is a mistake. I love mediumship. Why me? Do I feel ill? I think I'm ill...*

'My daughter will be there.'

Clear as crystal, a man's voice cut through my inner yammering and I turned around to see where it came from, ready to apologize for muttering out loud. But there was no one there – and I hadn't been speaking aloud. I stood, rooted to the spot in disbelief, before the realization dawned that I was a medium and that this madness was normal.

I tentatively began to walk and the man's commentary continued:

'... my daughter, Catherine. And that's where I used to live... and this is the church I went to all my days.'

I could feel him pointing inside my mind, drawing my attention this way and that, first down a narrow side street and then to a beautiful Gothic church across the road.

'I had a terrible lung disease,' he continued. 'Everybody did their best. Catherine did her best. I know that. Will you tell Catherine I know that? It's her father, Thomas.' I could feel his intention – stoic, West-of-Scotland tenderness.

'I certainly will, sir,' I promised, whispering out loud.

After that, the hours flew by like minutes and, before I knew it, I was waiting outside the spiritualist church in the rain. I was shown into the building and took my seat on the platform – an area like a stage in front of the congregation where the medium and the chairperson sit. There were candles, angel ornaments and a thin hymn book in front of me. I was engaged in silent panic. I felt like I'd turned up for Sunday lunch in my bathing suit – out of place, drawing attention, silly, vulnerable and inappropriate.

I was panicking so badly that my mind had detached from my body and I felt like I was dreaming. It wasn't me up there.

I was sitting in the audience watching this young woman on the platform with sympathy as she sweated, trembled and grew paler by the minute.

The chairperson announced the opening prayer and I remembered that I *was* me. I was up there. I was the sweaty, pasty girl. And I had a job to do. There was no escaping it now.

I shakily stood up and said the prayer, avoiding eye contact with anyone – I still had no idea at this point if anyone in Spirit was there. I was so trapped in the confines of my own self-consciousness that a stampede of elephants couldn't have got through to me. And yet here I was, hoping for the subtle impression of a nonphysical person through the internal cacophony.

After the opening prayer there were some hymns, a reading and some intimations, all of which provided me with just enough time to get myself into a right old state before getting up to perform one of the most miraculous, sensitive, frightening and important tasks of my life.

'Lauren will now give us her demonstration of mediumship,' said the chairperson.

My legs were like jelly and the room was packed with silent, expectant faces.

You could have heard a fairy's pin drop.

My mind raced and flipped and flopped with fear – searching for something to say to get me through this embarrassment. And I couldn't have felt further away from Spirit. But one thought kept coming to me, punctuating the random mental somersaults: the promise I'd made to the invisible man that I'd try to get a message to his daughter.

It's all I've got, I thought. And I meant it.

I had no idea how to formulate what had happened earlier in the day into a cohesive 'proper' message from Spirit, so I did the only thing I could think of. I told the story. I told it straight. I wasn't Lauren the majestic medium. I was just Lauren the 23-year-old woman, telling a story about her day.

'Earlier on today, the weirdest thing happened,' I said.

Silence.

'Hmm-hmm', I cleared my throat. 'I was walking home from doing a spot of shopping and I was accompanied by a gentleman… no, not in that way…'

A few chuckles from the audience.

'A gentleman in Spirit. An invisible man,' I went on. 'He joined me as I was walking up Paisley High Street, past the church. He told me he used to go to that church, and he pointed down Baker Street and told me he used to live there. He said his name was Thomas and that he'd had a terrible lung disease. He wanted to talk to his daughter, Catherine, and tell her how much he appreciated what she did for him. He was a quiet sort of man – loving, but quiet. I could tell he loved his daughter very much. I may have made all this up in my own mind, but I thought I'd mention it, just in case. I promised him I would.'

Silence.

I swallowed hard and stood in the stillness for what felt like 10 minutes, but was probably two seconds.

I began to turn away, disappointed that I'd made a mistake, when out of the corner of my eye I saw a hand slowly rise at the back of the room.

'I'm Catherine and my dad was Thomas. He died of asbestos-related complications and he lived right where you said, right down that street.'

The audience and I gasped. My eyes widened and my hand came to my mouth in shock. Catherine's eyes were filling up with tears and so were mine. And so were her father's.

From Fear to Love

I wanted to share this story to let you know that it's OK to be afraid in the course of developing your mediumship – but that fear is not a reason to stop, to hide at the back of the workshop or behind a computer. Spirit wants you to succeed in delivering the message even more than you do, and they will not leave you there alone if you are willing. It's OK to 'feel the fear and do it anyway', as American psychologist Susan Jeffers once wrote – your mediumship will still 'work', but what is even better is to get out of self-conscious fear and into a feeling of expansive, connected love when you do your thing. That, essentially, is the journey of personal growth we must undertake as mediums: to get out of fear and into love.

On this occasion, Spirit knew that I'd be so deep into fear in the moment that they had to get the message to me beforehand, when I was gazing at a beautiful church, relaxed and happy and about to live my dream of demonstrating mediumship for the first time – when I was in unself-conscious, expanded love. In the moment, the success of the message was down to the father and daughter's love for each other. Their love was stronger than my fear. And that night, up on that platform, I understood; I felt the significance of love in mediumship. Love was what made it possible for him to communicate with me. Love had brought his daughter to the spiritualist church on that dark, rainy night, love was what he wanted to talk about and it was his love for her that stuck with me – that gave me the words when I was silently flailing about up there like a fish out of water.

Spirit is always there. Spirit loves you. Spirit cannot be offended. Spirit is a raging river of information. Spirit is always guiding you – pushing on your awareness, trying to pop through into your consciousness. Spirit is the Great Intelligence in which all other intelligences bloom. Spirit cannot 'leave' you because all of existence is Spirit and you are Spirit. Spirit is in every moment of the past, in the spaces between moments and gives energy to the unfolding of the future – a future that is already known to the Great Intelligence. Spirit is always ready and willing to work through you, powerfully. Everyone you've ever loved is both a child of and a contributor to this Infinite Great Intelligence. The imprint they have left can never be undone, and that imprint is part of you since you also are a child and co-creator of the Great Knowing. And whilst you may never have met, physically, the people in Spirit who will speak through you, you share the same powerful, expansive and eternal Mind.

Dismantling the Dam

If you experience communication with Spirit as a trickle (or not at all), it's because you've built a dam, and that dam is holding back the river. But what could be so powerful as to hold back a river like this?

The answer is the most powerful force in the universe: your thoughts, your beliefs, your emotions.

Our thoughts and beliefs are incredibly strong, and most of us have spent a lifetime building up a dam of beliefs designed to staunch the flow of Spirit and keep us focused on the physical world, our individuality and, sadly, our inadequacies.

The way to become an extraordinary medium is to begin to deconstruct the dam – brick by brick, thought by thought, belief by belief.

The analogy of the dam is helpful in explaining how I could be in such fear and panic, so inexperienced, and yet a wonderful, accurate and loving message was able to make it through the dam of doubtful, fearful beliefs I'd constructed.

Often, when I coach my students, we find that one key brick – one limiting, damaging, fearful belief – is holding the whole thing up. And as soon as we chisel it out and expose it as false, the whole dam comes crashing down and, overnight, their connection with Spirit becomes a powerful, consistent flow.

What's important is just to begin: to be OK with being a beginner and to get to work on that first brick. Usually, the first brick looks like fear of judgement, fear of ridicule, fear that you're not good enough, the thought that you're not psychic, the feeling of discomfort that what you're about to experience, share or say is not OK/not valid/not valuable. But it's just one brick. And if you can tackle it and remove it, more information from Spirit will begin to get through.

There are many, many, potentially excellent mediums out there who never even make it out the starting block because they don't get past that first brick – the fear of being a beginner. *Beginner's luck* is real. Often, those first few messages we give from Spirit, when we have no expectation and we're willing to try and see what happens, are awesome, thrilling and life-changing both for the recipient and the medium.

And then it goes away.

It goes away because Spirit wants to show you what you are capable of, and then invites you to go on a journey of discovery to learn *how* you did it. That's what we're doing here in this book – helping you walk the path that will allow you to be free of the hesitation and fear that prevent the Truth of Spirit from flowing through your heart, your mind and out of your mouth in a way that heals and comforts others. The journey is designed to help you become both a more free-flowing medium and a more free-flowing person; they are one and the same thing.

If you have intuitive/spiritual experiences and you're interested in developing, then that's all that's needed for you to begin. Don't overthink it. Even the best mediums in the world started as beginners.

Allow yourself to begin each reading, each demonstration, each meditation, and each stage of your development in a spirit of love, self-discovery, service and enthusiasm and you won't go wrong. The only way you won't develop is if you don't develop – so just begin!

In the previous chapter, we worked on cultivating certain qualities that exist in all great mediums. I have also touched on the idea that your work with Spirit is a reflection of who you are, and I'd like to explain more about what I mean by that now.

Mediumship is a collaboration between you and Spirit. Spirit cannot give more to you than you give to yourself. This entails the following:

- Spirit is limited by how limited you believe you are.

- Your mediumship can only be as impactful as you believe you deserve to be.

- The kind of information that comes is the kind that you're comfortable with.

- Miracles happen in your mediumship only when you believe miracles are possible.

- Your mediumship is as valuable as you believe you are.

The Role of Love in Mediumship

There are many different kinds of love, but they all seem to have one thing in common: someone is doing the loving and someone, or something, is being loved – whether you love your partner, your dog, your creator or that chocolate bar you simply can't say no to in the supermarket. *Love*, then, describes a kind of relationship between things. Therefore, when we speak of love, we're really speaking about relationships.

Mediumship is also about relationships. It's about the relationship between a father and his daughter, a son and his mother, sisters, friends, lovers, companions and owners and their pets, to name just a few.

I used to think that the relationship between a person in Spirit and their living relative was enough to carry the message, and it didn't matter what *I*, as the medium, thought or felt, since I was only passing the message along. I now understand that if communication through a medium is to be healing for all concerned, it does matter what the medium thinks and feels – because they are a part of the relationship too, if only for a short time.

It is said that the way you do one thing is the way you do everything. If that is to be believed, then the kinds of relationships we mediums experience in our lives will be reflected in our mediumship.

In short, becoming conscious of the quality of our relationships, and choosing to become more loving and more loved will enable us to better fulfil our roles as mediums.

Let us first discuss the most important relationship of all: the relationship you have with yourself.

Love Yourself, Strengthen Your Mediumship

Any time my mediumship has been crappy (hey, it happens) it's been because something in my life triggered me to believe that I wasn't good enough, and so I shouldn't love myself. For example, I may have seen a news item that made me feel afraid. I'd think, *I need to do more*; *I should give more to charity*; *maybe I should volunteer*; *how can I fix this?* So although I'd only glanced at the news item on TV, I'd made it mean that *I* wasn't doing enough, and *I* wasn't good enough – and so *I* wasn't deserving of love. Can you relate to this?

Whether you're not losing weight as fast as you think you should be, or you feel guilty about the way you've parented your kids, or you haven't managed to keep the house immaculately clean and tidy – if you're being super-hard on yourself about how you're progressing in life, and you're turning your circumstances into an indication that you're not deserving of love, then this is going to have a detrimental effect on your mediumship.

But in order to bring compelling, accurate and healing evidence through, you must believe that you *are* good enough. You need to *increase* feelings of love, compassion and acceptance towards yourself to have a positive effect on your work with Spirit.

We looked at loving ourselves more in the previous chapter in our discussion about the qualities of a medium. Investing time, energy and attention in developing those qualities within yourself is an act of self-love. Even admitting that you already possess some of these qualities is acknowledgement of yourself in a loving way. As much as possible, keep yourself pointed in the direction of self-awareness, self-acceptance, self-compassion and self-investment. Do not entertain shameful and accusing thoughts that make you feel not good enough and unloved. And if you find yourself stuck, refer back to 'The Anatomy of a Medium' (*see page 39*), and spend some time contemplating how far you've come in cultivating the requisite qualities, then think about what you can do next to encourage feelings of love and kindness towards yourself.

Your Significant Relationships

When you have loving feelings towards yourself, it makes it a whole lot easier to give and receive love in your significant relationships, as well as to forgive and accept others. And when you feel relaxed with the people around you, and connected to them in a loving way, you will experience the same feelings of calm and connection when you work with people in your mediumship.

The information will flow from Spirit more clearly and more easily, you'll experience less self-doubt, you'll be able to express yourself more easily, and your mediumship will be a vessel for deep healing because it will be infused with love. You won't feel self-conscious about how people perceive you or worry about what they think because you'll be too focused on being of service.

What's the Alternative?

When we don't feel good enough, and we don't feel loved, we feel fear. In our relationships with ourselves, this often takes the form of anxiety, addiction and myriad forms of mental conflict. When we're afraid in our personal relationships, we often feel that we have to protect or defend ourselves, lashing out or withdrawing in an attempt to escape pain.

Just as our experience with loving relationships transfers itself onto our mediumship, our experiences with conflict, pain and fear do too. Feeling not good enough and not loved is a sure way to feel disconnected from Spirit and unsure of yourself in your mediumship. If you come to give a message from Spirit, and it's difficult, or the information is inconsistent, or it's lacking transformative emotional impact, it would be wise to look at whether you're feeling not good enough and not loved in your relationship with yourself, and whether that's being reflected in any of your personal relationships too. If you can identify the source of the feeling, and correct it, your mediumship will grow stronger.

Returning to Love

If you're experiencing frustration in your mediumship, and you know it's because you feel not good enough and therefore, not loved, you can find immediate relief by identifying and interrupting the thought that's causing the feeling. I usually say something like 'No!' or 'Stop!' when I catch myself beginning to spiral. I then put one hand on my heart, breathe deeply and say or think, 'I love and accept myself completely'. This may seem like a 'quick fix', but for me, it's become a habit, and through this habit, I've begun to default to having loving thoughts towards myself. Not only does it feel so much better to think kindly of myself, and be a friend to myself, but it has helped me to be more confident and open in my relationships with people in Spirit and their living relatives too.

Loving Bad Spirits

I receive several e-mails per month from people who have mediumistic experiences but are afraid to explore or develop them in case they encounter 'bad spirits'. I have never, in my years as a medium, come across a bad spirit. And I think that's because I don't believe in them. What I do believe is that we all have a light side and a shadow side, and when we pass to Spirit, the complexity of our personalities and the lives we lived goes with us. The kindest person you know has the capacity to be cruel and the cruellest person you can think of was once an innocent baby with no say in their genetics or early-life influences.

You, as the medium, get to choose the kind of Spirit personalities you want to align with by choosing your own mindset. Those you connect with are a reflection of some aspect of your own self, your own beliefs and your own relationship to fear and love. If you believe you are deeply troubled and fearful, then your mental mediumship will be deeply troubled and fearful. If you are loving and open-hearted, and you believe in the good in others, then that will be your experience of Spirit. This is why your personal-development journey is key to the quality and healing impact of your mediumship – because it's your responsibility, as the medium, to be someone who confidently handles love, knows what healing feels like, is equipped to believe in the good in others and in their own worthiness as a conduit for it. That is what will make your mediumship exceptional. Your childhood may not have been perfect: you may have been starved of love; there may have been someone who was cruel to you; you may have had to protect and defend yourself; you may believe, deep down, that you are bad and that people are bad; you may have grown up looking for warning signs that an argument was about to blow up at home; or you may have been raised watching too many horror movies. If you have not healed your beliefs around these experiences, they will colour your mental mediumship, so that you feel you relate best to 'bad spirits' and your understanding is of the shadow side of people, rather than the light side.

If, on the other hand, you are prepared to believe in love, able to forgive and to focus on happy memories and you care for yourself and for others and realize that they care for you – if these are the things you give energy to in life, then this will be your experience of Spirit.

Imagine yourself as a transmitter and receiver of waves of consciousness, and you have a dial that you can tune from fear right through to love and all the channels in between. You get to decide which channel to tune yourself into, and you will receive information on that wavelength from Spirit. 'Bad spirits' can be found on the channel 'fear'. If you don't want to receive them, you have to tune yourself out of that channel. Sounds easy enough, right? But it can be a lifelong commitment to stop yourself slipping back into it, especially if you experienced a lot of fear in your early life. It can take many attempts to tune yourself into forgiveness, innocence and love if you've spent a lot of time being afraid.

Let's take Julie, for example. Julie's dad used to hit her

mother, abused her and then left when she was six years old and never came back. As an adult, Julie has realized that she has mediumistic abilities, but she's worried about 'bad spirits' – not because she's ever seen one, but because her early life experience told her people are bad and that hurt and negativity are more powerful than love and goodness. So she is afraid to develop her awareness for fear that she'll attract the 'strongest' Spirit – and the strongest spirit she knows of (meaning the experience that affected her most) is harm and negativity from her father. In order to transform this belief and realize that love is powerful, strong and all around her in Spirit, she's going to have to do some work on forgiveness, cultivating love, acceptance and understanding that she is a strong force of love herself.

She may have to explore where there is love in what happened with her father. This is no easy task, but if she can see the lesson or the blessing that came as a result of his behaviour, and if she can find compassion for herself, and for him, she will see that she has the power to transform her fears into love, and that there are no bad spirits, just as there are no bad people – we are all both, and now she gets to choose to connect with the loving side of people, and the loving side of Spirit. Doing all of this will tune her to a different channel.

If you, like Julie, fear bad spirits, this is an invitation for you to explore whether you fear bad people, and for you to heal and transcend the fears that may be there.

☆ ACTIVATION 7 ☆

Changing the Channel from Fear to Love

The following exercise is an intimate, revealing and intense one that you must complete with the utmost kindness and compassion towards yourself. As you become aware of your subconscious thoughts and fears, they may be released and healed. By shining the light of awareness on whatever may have been in the dark, you expose and diminish it, and it ceases to frighten you. Be patient with the process and really give some careful thought to these questions:

- From age 0–12 who did you fear?

- When did you learn to be wary of people?

- What is the lesson or the blessing in that experience?

- What was great about it?

- What was great about the person who taught you to be wary?

- What's not perfect about him/her yet?

- What will it take for you to forgive them?

- Can you decide to forgive them now?

- What will it be like to be free of pain and fear? Who will you be? What will you do?

When you explore the above questions, you will train yourself to become someone who can see the love in any situation, the innocence in any perpetrator and find compassion no matter what. Then you won't have to worry about bad spirits any more because you will realize that they don't exist, and that if love can be found in any situation, then only love can be real.

Find the love, and you will have shone light into the darkness. It's like riding a bike: when you've done it once, you'll always know how to do it.

Meditation is the key to developing powerful, accurate, healing and miraculous mediumship, lifting your awareness up and out of the maze of beliefs that cause you to feel a less loving mental or emotional state, such as fear, anger or worry. It offers you a bird's-eye view of those beliefs, thereby giving you the choice – do you want to believe them or not? – helping you to see that they are not actually part of you. This realization alone can be powerful.

Meditation also trains you to listen to the subtle cues of your mind, body, senses and emotions. By closing your eyes, you are no longer 'in' your body. Your awareness expands out of your 'self' and it's in this area of expansion that you and Spirit will blend and you will become aware of information, thoughts and feelings that are not your own, forming the basis of your mental mediumship.

If a one-to-one sitting or a platform demonstration is the marathon, then meditation is training for that marathon.

There are so many benefits to meditation, both for you personally and for your mediumship, that I wholly and completely recommend that you make it a part of your daily life.

☆ ACTIVATION 8 ☆

Reaching Out to Spirit Meditation
(Shining the Light of Awareness)

This meditation is a variation of one called 'Sitting in the Power'. You can follow it here or you can listen to it by visiting this page on my website: www.laurenrobertson. co.uk/mim/meditation2.

Prepare by ensuring your meditation space is peaceful and relaxed. You might want to tidy up a little bit, burn your favourite incense or light some candles. At the very least, ensure that pets and people are out of the room and that you won't be disturbed. Wear clothing that is comfortable and loose-fitting or be naked, if you like – it's entirely up to you.

- Sit comfortably on a supportive chair or on the floor in a cross-legged position – or you can lie down, if you prefer. Place your hands, palms facing the sky, in the spirit of receiving. Close your eyes and, as you do so, take a deep, nourishing breath and feel it fill your whole body with oxygen.

- Take a few more slow, deep breaths in and out, and feel your body becoming more and more relaxed. Feel muscles you didn't know you had begin to release and relax, and the more relaxed you become, the more you focus on your inner space.

- Continue to breathe through your nose, normally and deliberately, and bring your awareness to your solar plexus, where a white flame of life burns – the light of your existence, your Divine Spark.

- Every time you take a breath, the oxygen causes your Divine Spark to expand until the light of you fills your entire body: from your head to your toes, from the very tip of the fingers on one hand to those on the opposite one – you are filled with light.

- Now, as you take another deep breath, your light pops outside the parameters of your body, enveloping you and encircling you, creating a beaming aura of white light that emanates from within you and surrounds you. Your light gently expands and contracts with your breathing. Take a moment to enjoy the sensation of expansion, connection and power.

- Using your awareness, your intention, you can control and influence your light. Imagine, then, that your aura has fingers that can touch and feel the world around you as you remain still with your eyes closed.

- From the front of your body, the front of your aura, send your fingers of light out, out, farther, farther, touching everything in their path, until they reach the farthest point of the room in front of you. The light stays as you bring your awareness back to your centre.

- Now send your fingers of light out your back – farther, farther, touching everything in their path until you reach the farthest point of the room at your back. The light stays as you bring your awareness back to your centre.

- Send your fingers of light out to your left side now – reaching, touching, feeling everything in their path until they reach the farthest point of the room. The light stays as you bring your awareness back to your centre.

- And now to your right – send your light out, touching, stroking, feeling and sensing everything in its path. The light stays and your awareness returns to your centre.

- Send your light downwards now – feel the floor underneath you. Spread your light out everywhere until you've covered the entire floor, and bring your awareness back to your centre.

- Upwards now, with outstretched light, send your awareness up and out, stretching up, up, feeling the temperature of the air as you do – spreading all across the ceiling until the light joins up with the others, covering and filling the whole room with your awareness.

- Take a moment to enjoy this feeling of expansion. Say the following words in your mind or out loud: 'My light is a beacon that calls in only love. I call to Spirit, I connect with Spirit, I empathize with Spirit. I know that I am safe, that I am powerful, that I am loved. When I send this light outside of myself, I invite the awareness of others in Spirit. Of my own loved ones, and of those who would bring a message of love to their living relatives. When I access this sacred space of light, I can know anything about anyone at any time.'

- Take a few moments to bask in the loving glory of your spirit – like sunlight touching skin. Take your time to absorb any wisdom that comes to you now. Cherish feelings of love, compassion and forgiveness as they arise. Be filled with feelings of power, energy and enthusiasm as you sense the loving presence of Spirit all around you.

- As you become satiated, return gently to your body, to your breathing, to the points where your body meets a surface. Bring yourself back to you, to the room around you, to the temperature of your skin, to the noises outside.

- When you feel ready, wiggle your fingers, wiggle your toes (knowing that your light burns still) and open your eyes.

For best results, do this meditation daily. Make notes in your journal about any changes, feelings, awareness that you have.

☆ Activation 9 ☆
An Increase in Love

Imagine that there is a golden telephone with a golden line. The better the golden phone is maintained and the more conductive threads there are in the golden line, the more clearly you can hear the person on the other end. Imagine, now, that the only thing that repairs, strengthens and fortifies the golden line is the feeling of love in those making and receiving the call. The golden line is your mediumship and every time you feel love towards yourself and others you strengthen your connection.

If you're anything like me, you want to be the best, clearest and most loving medium you can be. The following exercise will help you to invite more love into your life in order to achieve this.

A word to the wise before we proceed: love comes in many forms and, often, unloving thoughts, feelings and actions that have long grown wild in the garden of your mind have to be uprooted before the soil can hold love in its place. So sometimes the quest to increase love can be painful. It may involve forgiveness, releasing old anger that has kept you company for a long time, admitting you were wrong, apologizing, accepting someone else's apology, accepting a compliment, saying no when you'd usually say yes, saying yes to yourself and your desires when you'd usually say no and all other manner of irregular and unfamiliar feelings, thoughts and actions.

Increasing the amount of love in your life is not a fluffy-unicorn pastime. It's work, and it requires a depth of introspection, self-awareness and honesty that many fear to venture into because it means a lot of change and transformation. But change is part of life and transformation is Divine, and when we take away the unloving thoughts and feelings that have accompanied us for years and replace them with love, it can only be positive, both in our lives and in our mediumship.

Begin by making some sacred and nurturing time to take stock of the amount of love in your life. Create time, space and surroundings that will feel conducive to the process.

In your journal, answer the following questions at length. If you need to take a break, fine, but please try to complete them in one sitting to ensure continuity in your state of mind and to really anchor the transformational healing power that comes from focusing on love.

1. What are you doing and being when you feel the strongest feelings of love in your life?

2. Who are you with when you feel the strongest feelings of love?

3. What are you doing and being when you feel the weakest feelings of love in your life?

4. Who are you with when you feel love only weakly?

5. When you were a child, whose love did you try to win – your mother's or your father's?

6. What role did you have to perform to gain love from your mother or father?

7. In what way is that search for love and the role you played to get it still playing out in your life today?

8. Who has held love away from you?

9. What could you do to love that person more?

10. In a given situation, put your hand on your heart and ask yourself this question: what is the most loving thing to do in this situation? Now act on it. Do the loving thing your heart knows to do, even when there are easier/more familiar/more indulgent options available.

Increasing the amount of love in my life by asking myself these questions and acting on them, where possible, has improved the quality of my mediumship dramatically. I think this is because when I am filled up with love, I don't need the approval of my recipient or audience. I become free to say what's really there, and available for the truest impressions from Spirit. When I'm in a good place with myself – when I'm squared up emotionally with things going on in my own life – I don't care about looking like a fool and making a mistake. I'm free and available to be of service because my needs are met.

Try it for a few weeks and see the difference it makes to your connection with Spirit.

CHAPTER HIGHLIGHTS

★ It's normal to feel anxious, nervous or afraid when practising your mediumship. These feelings are not a reason to stop. Embrace them and continue.

★ Increasing feelings of love in your life will strengthen your mediumship.

★ There is no such thing as bad spirits – they are an illusion that show us where there's room to love more.

★ Sometimes love is challenging. Real love can require that you release the fear, bitterness, anger or blame that have kept you company for a long time. Freedom in your life – and in your mediumship – is on the other side of that release.

CHAPTER 6

THE GREAT INTELLIGENCE

I chuckled as I plucked a folded raffle ticket from the large glass bowl.

'Are they giving out prizes, do you think?' I asked my mum, as we made our way into the sanctuary of the Arthur Findlay College for Psychic Studies along with 100 other mediums from around the world.

'Perhaps,' she smiled.

We took our seats, all crammed in and laughing excitedly like psychic sardines on holiday. Then the crescendo tailed off and we grew quiet, as my mentor, Paul Jacobs, made his way to the platform to begin his lecture on the importance of proving the intelligence of Spirit. I listened intently as Paul described the intersection of Spirit and science. He explained the importance of proving that during a sitting or public demonstration, the medium is connecting with the intelligence of the person in Spirit, and that the way to do this is to remove all other sources from which the medium might be obtaining information. By eliminating the possibility that the medium has judged the recipient's clothing or appearance to come to certain conclusions or that they've picked up clues from the recipient's voice or they are reading them psychically, we give weight to the conclusion that they must be getting their information from a third intelligence – that of the person in Spirit whose essence and awareness has continued on.

'Lauren,' he declared.

I shot back to the room at the sound of my name. I'd been miles away, listening to what he was saying, whilst thinking of all the different experiments I could devise to prove the intelligence of Spirit.

'Lauren.'

I looked up and he was indeed speaking to me.

'Would you care to come and demonstrate the intelligence of Spirit?'

No I would not. I would not care to at all, I thought.

'Yes Paul, of course,' I heard myself say, as my body began to get up without my permission.

My heart beat hard against my ribcage as I felt the eyes of 100 mediums boring into the back of my head, afraid for me and, at the same time, wishing me well. My jelly legs and I stepped up onto the platform, my raffle ticket crushed and pulpy in my now sweaty hand. I crammed it into the pocket of my jeans, turned to face the audience and gave Paul a frightened smile.

'What I'd like you to do is turn around, with your back to the audience and pick a ticket from the bowl in front of you. You will then read the number aloud, at which time the owner of the counterpart to that ticket will identify themselves to me. You will then use your mediumship to give evidence of the continued existence of their loved ones in Spirit, and I will answer 'yes' or 'no' on the recipient's behalf in response to the information that you give. The raffle tickets have been chosen at random, and you will be blindfolded, so that you will be unable to see or hear the person you are reading for or receive visual cues of any kind. Is that understood?'

I nodded meekly and looked at the bowl of raffle tickets. As I moved to make my selection, I noticed number 33 with its face pressed against the glass, near the rear of the bowl. I like repetitive numbers, so I dug down and caught it in a pincer grip.

'Read it aloud,' Paul commanded.

'Number 33,' I croaked.

At this point, the rear wall of the platform, vases of lilies and the glass bowl of tickets were all plunged into darkness as a blindfold descended softly over my eyes.

I vaguely remember some shuffling and scuffling at my back as the owner of ticket number 33 was identified.

I have never in my whole life prayed so hard and with such desperation. I was convinced this was never going to work. How could I possibly give a message if I didn't know who the recipient was? I was scared of making a fool of myself, and the only solution I could think of was to pray. Hard. *Please God and People-In-Spirit, be with me up here and I'll be good for the rest of my life. Please don't leave me standing up here alone. Please let love and truth come through my words and I promise I'll be the most exemplary woman ever – in your name which is light. Amen. Pretty Please.*

'The owner of ticket 33 has been identified, Lauren – please begin. Give only one piece of information at a time, so the recipient can confirm if it is accurate or not. Understood?'

'Understood,' I squeaked.

I was in full-blown panic mode. I was staring at the inside of the blindfold and my eyelids, hoping for X-ray vision, or for the ground to swallow me up. I felt tight, constricted and small.

'I see a woman,' I lied. 'I think it's Mum. Is your mother in Spirit?' I guessed.

'No,' Paul asserted.

My face screwed up under the blindfold and I knew I had to find a way to calm myself down. I took a deep breath. *I'm here to be of service*, I thought. *This isn't about me. I'm ready to receive.* A split second later, I was spontaneously enveloped by the strangest feeling of calm, and for a few moments nothing else happened. Then, suddenly, the darkness parted and I was no longer standing blindfolded in the sanctuary, but seated in a kitchen, amongst a family.

There were several children around me, lots of food on the table, the feel of the polished, wooden table under my fingertips. I sensed a beloved, elderly lady, a scarf around my neck and the feeling of belonging. It felt so long ago.

I began again.

'I have your grandmother here. Did you live with her?'

'Yes,' came Paul's voice, after the longest moment.

I counted the people around the table in my mind's eye. 'Are you a family of seven?'

'Yes.'

'Your grandmother has just placed a scarf around my neck – did she give this to you as a gift?'

'Yes,' Paul responded. 'And make this the last piece of information, Lauren.'

'You remember the feel of that table. It's mahogany: a big, oval mahogany table in the kitchen.'

'Yes. We sat around that very table as a family. Yes it was mahogany, yes it was oval,' Paul relayed.

I exhaled. My heart was beating hard and, as I returned to my seat, I was immediately filled with gratitude and amazement at the experience.

To this day, I have no idea who the recipient of the message was. What I do know is that I participated in an experiment that proved to me, beyond doubt, the reality of the continuation of our awareness and essence after death.

I held on to ticket number 33. I often look at it and smile, especially if I'm uncertain or fearful about my mediumship. And when I look at the ticket and remember what happened that day, I know for sure that our loved ones are with us, that our connection to Spirit is real and that I need not question myself, worry that I'm a fraud or fear I'm 'making it all up'.

I wanted to share this story with you in order to encourage you to embrace the scientific method and critical thinking as important elements for developing your mediumship and for strengthening its quality. Many mediums confuse scepticism and cynicism with the scientific method. But it is a perfectly helpful way for you to explore, test and record the results of your mediumship. And, as you've just read, it can be powerful in proving that what you do is real and that your mind is capable of so much. Don't be afraid to experiment with your practice and test it for accuracy. Doing so will make you a better medium and increase your confidence in your abilities.

Some mediums also confuse critical thinking with criticism. I don't mean that you should criticize yourself or your mediumship in an emotionally negative sense. Thinking critically is about examining your mediumship, reflecting on your performance, enquiring as to the accuracy or inaccuracy of the message, looking for what is true or false in your information, identifying what is fact and what is simply a belief and becoming clear about what helps you and what holds you back in your work. It's about asking why? How? What are the rules? How can I repeat this?

To develop excellence, athletes time themselves, record their calorie intake, do exercises that train their muscles and drop habits, thoughts and behaviours that don't serve them. They do this because both the athlete and his or her trainer have thought critically about what works and what doesn't. If you want to achieve excellence in your mediumship, so must you.

Why Are We Mediums?

For the purpose of elevating your confidence in your mediumship, I'd like to offer you my theory of *why* we have evolved to possess such an extraordinary ability and how mediumship is possible. I have developed these ideas over years of thinking critically about my ability to communicate true information about people who have died and whom I have never met. I hope that these explanations will help you to see that your mediumship is grounded in reality, so that you can move forwards in your work with Spirit with confidence and certainty.

As human beings, we have the features and qualities that we do as a result of genetic mutations that made us more successful as a species. These qualities are preserved and spread amongst our species through a process called natural selection over millions of years.

For the purpose of this discussion, let's take it as fact that human beings have the capacity to understand each other psychically, and that communication with Spirit is possible. In other words, let's assume we can become accurately aware of the personalities, events, memories and likenesses of people who are living and who have passed, without physically knowing them or being materially present for the events of their lives. If we are the result of natural selection, then we must possess these abilities because they are beneficial to the survival and success of our species. Just as a polar bear has evolved to have a thick, warm, white coat to keep it warm and camouflaged in the snow, so must our abilities improve our chances of thriving and surviving.

So what might be the benefit of being able to 'see' into the lives, minds, emotions, past, present and future of other people? In what way do these abilities help us to thrive and survive?

It is already widely accepted that we have an ability to look into the lives of others in a way that's beneficial to the survival of the human race: it's called empathy.

Empathy is defined as 'the ability to understand and share the feelings of another' and it's quite obvious why being able to do this would help the human race to survive. We are a species that depends on community and on each other, working together to keep society ticking along. So to be able to empathize with each other is essential. Understanding the feelings of another allows us to see them as being like us – having feelings like ours, the capacity to love as we do and to be hurt by the same things that hurt us. On a base, animalistic level, this allows us to procreate and look after our young and it prevents us from seeing our friends and family as threatening, which might lead to conflict and killing. We empathize with them – we understand their thoughts, feelings and actions as being like ours, and we assume they are motivated by the same things that motivate us – and so we don't hurt them or kill them. Instead, we love them, we feel their pain, we comfort them and we work together to survive.

After Empathy

Unfortunately, in this age, a rudimentary form of empathy is not enough. We are no longer animals whose only concerns are our immediate tribe and finding food, shelter and a mate. Across millions of years, we have developed higher mental faculties that have unlocked our imaginations and an awareness of self. Our lives and minds have become nuanced and complex – we have developed the ability to live out a story, reflect on it and deem it our *identity*, then make up more stories in our minds about what may happen in the future. We have become aware, not just of our base instincts, but of how the world is and our place within it, beyond our local tribe. We can look up at the stars and wonder. We can look at each other and question. We can look at the past and judge. We can imagine the future and worry.

So if we're going to continue to survive and thrive, we *must* evolve to possess a version of empathy that is appropriate for our complex and nuanced minds and societies. Up until very recently, the dangers and illnesses that could kill us were limited by our geography. And the amount of care and love we were expected to give was limited by the number of people we had direct access to (our immediate family and tribe). Relatively new inventions – penicillin, air travel and the internet – have meant that things that would commonly have killed us in the past are no longer a threat, whilst the number of people we feel emotionally connected to has increased exponentially. The internet has allowed us to be omnipresent, but with brains that are used to caring only for our tribe we're struggling to cope. We have to evolve and increase our capacity to care, in response to the number of people we now have to care for. One way in which I believe we are doing this is through an increased sensitivity to the thoughts and feelings of others: the evolved kind of empathy has to include intuitive abilities such as mediumship.

I argue, then, that our intuition, psychic abilities and capacity for mediumship are *empathy* evolved. These capacities help us to understand and live up to our responsibilities in an increasingly complex world. Most of the problems we experience as human beings, both on an interpersonal and a global scale, are due to a lack of understanding, empathy and compassion for the feelings of others.

The End of Tribalism

When a 'tribe' or group appears not to share our beliefs, outlook and values, we view them as 'different', as antagonists and a potential threat, and so we become enemies. Our caveman brains insist that we must ensure the survival of our own tribe, and any threat to it must be extinguished. But these ancient urges no longer serve us, for two reasons.

First, we are no longer tribes in a way that is relevant to these urges, nor do we face the dangers they evolved to address.

Second, acting on the fear of death and the pain of loss – as if we are one tribe against another – is the basis of the world's problems now, and is at odds with the direction we are moving in. We currently enjoy global travel and communication; we will soon have a global currency. And yet, we are still acting as if other people in other places are our enemies. This is incompatible with a cooperative global community and makes no sense. I think that mediumship – because it is based on the principle that we are all connected and share so much in common – is one tool that will help us to transcend this contradiction, so that we can move into an age of cooperation, rather than antagonism. Because beyond our differing appearances and beliefs, we all want the same things for ourselves: love, peace, freedom, and to thrive.

The evolution of our intuitive abilities is enabling us to understand and share the feelings of others. We have developed the ability to *see* their circumstances, *feel* their pain, *hear* what they hear and *think* what they are thinking. In being able to perceive, mentally, the sorrow and joy of strangers as if they are our own, we begin to see them as part of our own tribe, and are more inclined to act lovingly towards them. Thus, our desire to fight them and protect ourselves from them is diminished.

The psychic with the flashing neon palm outside her shop, the medium developing his abilities in circle every week and you, who have picked up this book and read so far, are custodians of the empathy and compassion that will see the cessation of war and the salvation of our planet. It may take time, but your evolved sense of empathy and ability to interact with others from this place of deeper understanding spreads connection, love and forgiveness, little by little, every time you use them. And one day, the scales will tip, conflict will stop and cooperation will begin.

You have a very important job to do. If you think you're just giving a little message from Gran in Spirit that's of little consequence except to the person sitting before you, think again.

Transcending Labels

There is a stigma attached to the words 'psychic' and 'medium'. Furthermore, they no longer convey the full extent of our blossoming empathic abilities, which ought to be taken a lot more seriously than they currently are. So I'm going to give them a different name throughout the remainder of this chapter. I'm going to call our evolved abilities *phenomenological empathy* and I'll explain why.

Phenomenology is a word I learned at university when studying philosophy of mind. It means (loosely) *the philosophical study of the contents of consciousness.*

The contents of your consciousness include all your life experiences, your memories, your feelings, your hopes and dreams, language, your imagination, everyone you've ever known and loved, the colour red, that man over there, the texture of the seat underneath you and that dream you had about being naked on stage. The contents of your consciousness are *what it's like to be you.*

It has long been thought that this realm of first-person experience is completely private to you – that it is subjective and inaccessible to anyone else. Imagine you and your best friend go to a Hay House live event together. You sit side by side, watching and listening to your favourite speaker, and afterwards, you have a discussion over coffee about what each of you took from the talk. Your friend might remember 'A, B, C', of which you have no recollection, whilst you were most struck by 'X, Y, Z', which went completely over your friend's head. Has this ever happened to you? This is an example of how your first-person experience of the world is unique and private to you. But what if we are evolving so that the 'locked-off' worlds of our private minds are unlocking? What if we *are* able to access the contents of someone else's consciousness and get a glimpse of what it's like to be them? This is what I mean by *phenomenological empathy*. And this is what I think is occurring when we demonstrate what we currently call 'psychic abilities'.

When it comes to mediumship, we have to take our explanation a little further because we're talking not only about seeing into the mind of another person, but into the mind of someone who's no longer materially present with us. What's the evolutionary value of this ability? And even if it was advantageous, how could such a thing be possible?

The Evolutionary Function of Mediumship

Let's remain with the idea that we've evolved into phenomenologically empathic beings – humans with psychic abilities. Our abilities serve to ensure the survival of our species by helping us understand each other better, and in so doing we reduce feelings of fear and antagonism and increase feelings of peace, love and connection. It seems to me that if we are evolving past the fear of other tribes, we must also be evolving past the fear of harm and death, as well as the fear of the pain of loss.

I wrote in an earlier chapter that mediumship isn't wholly about the person who's passed coming to let us know that they are OK, but it's about the healing power that communication has for those of us still living.

If it's true that we continue to exist in some form after bodily death, then it follows that:

1. we do not need to fear our own death

2. we do not need to grieve the permanent loss of love, or of a loved one.

Our minds are evolving to enable us to perceive this truth, so that our behaviour will adapt in the direction of love and cooperation, rather than fear and conflict. There was a time in the history of humanity when fearing death was the smartest thing you could do. Those who feared death and took care to avoid harm survived and bore children. Fast forward many generations and *we* are their children, and the genes for 'fearing death' are alive and well in most of us, having been passed on to us by our ancestors.

But this fear is no longer appropriate. It contributes to our sense of separation and tribal antagonism. In the age in which we now live it is more evolutionarily advantageous for us to perceive and believe that we *don't* die – because if we don't die, then we don't have to be afraid that others might harm us, and we therefore have the ability to be loving, empathic and compassionate instead of fearful of our own demise. I argue, then, that mediumship is a naturally selected response to our changing social conditions, beyond the tribe, towards a global community. Nature has given us the means to stop fearing death, so that we may cooperate and help each other live fully.

The Mind of the Medium, the Mind of Spirit

The questions still remain: *how* is awareness of the personalities of people who have died (both our own loved ones and others') possible? How is awareness of past events that we ourselves were not physically present for possible? And what would have to be true for such awareness and communication to take place?

In all honesty, I don't know the answers. What I do know, from my own experience and critical thought about my mediumship, is that the phenomenology of you – the life experiences, awareness, memories, emotions and personality that make you who you are – somehow remains coherent and 'knowable' after you die.

It is as if our identities remain in the Great Intelligence. We cannot stop existing once we have existed in consciousness. Something of us remains, like magnetic clouds in the sky of the Great Intelligence.

I can just about comprehend how this could be so because even when I think my thoughts, I am aware of them. I am not them; I can pull my awareness away from them and observe them objectively. So my thoughts are the contents of my awareness, like clouds passing in the sky, and so I have no choice but to conclude that I am not only my body, I am not only my identity and I am not only my thoughts, but that each of these are the contents of a wider awareness. So when we die our identities remain, like clouds in the sky of the Great Intelligence.

You can develop your mediumship, so that it is no more difficult to identify a Spirit communicator than it is to look up and admire the clouds in the sky. I believe that mediumship is the result of the mind of the medium observing the phenomenological identity of a person in Spirit – the medium looks past her own identity clouds and is able to observe and describe other clouds in detail, as they make their way across the sky.

Testing Your Mediumship

You will especially enjoy the exercises in this chapter if you are willing to embrace critical thinking and the scientific method. A couple of experiments can be done on your own; many of them require a partner or a group. So if you are involved in a development circle, a workshop or another group environment where you can work on your mediumship, please feel free to use these experiments. Come and say hello in our Miraculous Mediumship Facebook Group, and share your results with our community.

In my experience, there are three powerful kinds of evidence of survival that we, as mediums, can transmit in our work. They are:

1. specific names, dates and factual details

2. intimate memories and private occurrences

3. mannerisms of a person in Spirit – for example, speech and posture.

The reason why these three categories are so powerful is because they're specific and compelling, and they evoke the true presence of the communicator. If you can achieve this level of intimacy and communication with a Spirit person, then your mediumship will be exceptional, miraculous and healing for your recipient and/or audience.

☆ ACTIVATION **10** ☆

Expressing the Communicator's Mannerisms

(Work with a partner)

This experiment will train you to receive a stronger sense of the communicator's mannerisms, posture, physical quirks, and the verbal expressions they used. When you're able to capture this as the medium, you bring the true essence of the person to the fore.

When a person in Spirit has come close enough for me to sense how they behaved, I've found myself patrolling the stage as a woman's father (a prison guard) once did; blowing my nose in a certain way (yes, in the middle of a demonstration); or doing a particular dance routine of which I had no previous knowledge, but which was performed regularly by an audience member's aunt – a professional dancer. If you too would like to bring forward this kind of evidence, try this:

- Sit face to face with your partner, and decide who will be A and who will be B. A will be the medium first and B should have a pen and paper to write with.

- Both of you close your eyes for a few minutes, gather your thoughts, give thanks to Spirit, and sit in the power if you haven't already (*see page 76*).

- B (recipient): your job is to send positive thoughts and loving feelings towards A, and soon, you will write down any looks, movements, words or mannerisms you see that could be relevant to one of your loved ones who've passed.

- A (medium): when you have prepared yourself and you feel the urge to do so, get up and move around the space. Stand, sit, make gestures, speak – do whatever you feel guided to do. The key here is not to be self-conscious about your movements or feel like you're controlling them or queuing messages up out of fear that you're not going to get anything, rather than being present in the moment. Be available to be carried by someone else's way of being and doing. Feel the impression of another influencing and guiding you as you float upon waves of awareness. Be available for different words, feelings, movements, noises and actions, but be spacious enough not to analyse or overwork them too much. Do this for about five minutes.

- All the while, B, you are to observe openly and make notes about what you see. Did any of your partner's words, actions or mannerisms resemble those of a loved one in Spirit?

- Finish up after five minutes and share your experiences. Give thanks. Reset your energy by closing your eyes and breathing intentionally for a few moments.

- B: now it's your turn. Let your inner Oscar winner go wild – act it out!

☆ ACTIVATION 11 ☆

Pushing the Boundaries of Accuracy and Insight

(Work with a partner or in a group)

How wonderful would it be to receive first names and surnames, specific dates, accurate and compelling memories and other specific information from Spirit, regularly and effortlessly?

You can achieve this, but before it can be easy and effortless, you have to break through your upper limit, your glass ceiling, your comfort zone – beyond what you currently believe is possible for you.

Like strenuous exercise, it's painful before it's easy. For this exercise, it's important to work with a partner or group you really trust – people with whom you can be comfortable being wrong and who won't judge you (because you *will* get it wrong... many times). A wise medium once told me that it's better to try for specific and clear information and get it wrong than to live in the land of vagueness where you get everything right (because it's so vague it could apply to anyone). I'm inclined to agree.

- As the medium, sit or stand facing your partner or group. Close your eyes and imagine that you are standing behind a beautiful red velvet curtain with gold ropes. This curtain is the only thing that separates you from all that is. Every piece of knowledge you could ever wish to receive is behind that curtain, just waiting to be perceived and known.

- Sit in your power (see the Reaching out to Spirit Meditation) and sense the presence of someone in Spirit with you. Begin your message and focus in on the details. If you find yourself thinking, *I'm not getting anything,* or feeling a bit stuck at any point throughout the message, go to the curtain and pull back the golden ropes in full trust that the information you seek will be on the other side.

- Now say exactly what you perceive there; don't hold back. You must force yourself to risk being wrong and desensitize yourself to the 'no'. Say exactly what you perceive there.

Practise this with several different partners and groups to increase your confidence and courage in going for the specific information and to retrain your mind to give itself access to the Great Intelligence. The more you can convince your mind to believe that you can see behind the curtain, that your mediumship can be accurate and that all the information you could ever want to know is right there waiting to be seen, the easier it will be to access.

When it's your turn to be the recipient/audience, keep track of how specific the medium is attempting to be, as well as anything he/she says that's spot-on accurate.

☆ ACTIVATION 12 ☆
The Power of the Unified Mind
(Work in a group)

It's my experience that Spirit uses the sum energy available during any instance of mediumship. The more people are on the same wavelength and of a similar mindset, the more energy is produced and the more successful the communication will be. The purpose of the next exercise, then, is to create a unified mind among the members of your development group, so that Spirit has a lot of energy to use.

You can either have one person lead the meditation verbally or listen to my recording of it, which can be found at www.laurenrobertson.co.uk/mim/meditation3. Or you can hold hands/link arms, so that you can feel the movement of the energy in the meditation silently, having listened to the instructions beforehand.

- Sit in a circle with your group and close your eyes.

- Bring your attention to your solar plexus and begin to ignite an orb or flame of energy there (your Divine Spark). Imagine the Divine energy travelling through your body and activating you with healing, loving, powerful light throughout.

- Now, begin to send your light to the person on your left. Start slowly, feel a little of your light move into them and a little of the light from the person on your right feeding into you.

- Again, a little faster now, the energy moves to the left.

- Faster still, with your eyes remaining closed, the energy moves around and around the circle – all colours, vibrations, perspectives and light blending and melding together as it moves faster and faster and faster around the circle, until it moves with such speed that it forms a solid white hoop of light that moves through you and around you, uniting you in mind, heart and intention with the members of your circle.

- When you feel ready, open your eyes and select one person from the group to sit in the centre. This person is the recipient and the rest of you are mediums.

- Use the collective energy you've created to each give a message to the recipient. There are three rules:

  1. Each message must be different, but can be related to another piece of evidence given.

  2. Each message must be less than 30 seconds long.

  3. Each message must be checked for accuracy by asking the recipient for yes/no confirmation.

☆ Activation 13 ☆
Think Outside the Book

(Work with a partner or in a group)

Spirit is everywhere and in everything and, if you let it, absolutely anything can help you connect the dots and get to the point of the message that a person in Spirit is trying to give you.

- Grab a random selection of books and place them, closed, on a table to the side.

- With your partner or group, close your eyes and say a little prayer, setting the intention that you will receive Divine and accurate information from Spirit through the words in the books.

- When it's your turn to be the medium, ask Spirit to guide you to one of the books. Pick it up and let yourself be guided to a page.

- Spend a few moments looking at the words on the page, and use them as a bridge between the communicator and you. Use the words in the book to inspire you and guide your message.

The point here is not to read the book; the point is to develop your awareness and sensitivity to the words you're being guided to, and trust that you are being guided by Spirit to what will best express their meaning.

For example, if you picked up *Red Gauntlet* by Sir Walter Scott (a book I read at university – just the first one that popped into my head) and you opened it at an intuitively selected page, you might read there about a principled man who worked hard and made his way up the ranks in the army. You may feel that this has been inspired by an uncle in Spirit who wishes to talk to his niece, and that he was a hard-working and principled man who was also in the army.

Try this a few times, and get lots of practice until you can clearly sense intuitively the direction, encouragement and 'nudges' Spirit gives you towards accurate information and meaning from the words and ideas in the book.

☆ Activation 14 ☆
Concentric Circles
(Work in a group)

The purpose of this exercise is twofold. First, it is for you to get lots of practice doing several mediumship communications in a row, without a break, so that your mind doesn't have the opportunity to get in the way and cause you to doubt. Second, it is designed for you to gather evidence of your ability to connect with the Great Intelligence in a 'blind' situation – where you cannot see the recipient.

This experiment works best with between 10 and 20 people, so if you are part of a large development group or workshop, this will be perfect for you. Divide the participants evenly between group A and group B. Group A should form a large circle, with each individual facing outwards, and group B should form a smaller circle inside circle A, so that every A person has a B person standing behind them, and every A person is facing away from their B partner, with B looking at the back of A's head. The As should not know who is standing behind them, so blindfolds may be a good idea. And make sure there is plenty of space between participants to avoid distraction.

Since the focus of this exercise is evidence, the Bs should have clipboards, so they can record the information that's given to them. The As are the mediums in this exercise.

- The group should take a moment to fall silent and go into their own place of power before all the As begin to connect with Spirit and give a message to the B person behind them. The Bs should say nothing at all to give their identity away, but simply take note of everything that is said to them by A.

- After a few minutes, indicate that the session has ended. All Bs should then move one place to the left, so that a different A is reading for them. Again, B should make notes, but say nothing. Continue like this until every A has given a message to every B. Now switch: the As are the recipients and the Bs are the mediums. Be sure to return to silent contemplation for a moment before switching to set the intention for who is the medium and who is the recipient.

When all As have given a message to all Bs, and then switched, so that all Bs have given a message to all As, and everyone has recorded the information they've received, re-form as a group and take a few moments to sort out the information that is accurate and correct, and who it came from.

You may wish to discuss your findings as a group – how each person felt, why some things were spot-on accurate, whether there are any patterns of information that were consistently accurate or inaccurate and what each participant learned from the experience.

This is an excellent exercise for building your confidence in working with different kinds of people and encouraging your mind to get into the 'flow' of information, rather than stopping, worrying or stalling about what to say. The pace of the exercise is so quick there isn't time to overthink it!

It is also a great way to prove the existence of the Great Intelligence of Spirit because in being unable to hear or see the recipient, the medium must rely only on what they receive from Spirit. Any correct and compelling evidence given during this kind of exercise makes it very difficult to doubt the integrity of the medium, to suggest they were 'hot' or 'cold' reading or even that they were picking up on subconscious cues from the recipients' age or clothing. 'Hot' reading implies that the medium is reading information about the communicator or the recipient, from some other source than the intelligence of the person in Spirit. 'Cold' reading implies that the medium is making statements and asking questions that are so vague anyone could say yes to them. Hot reading and cold reading are terms used by sceptics and cynics to imply that the medium is either deluded or dishonest. A medium who gathers evidence under these circumstances should treat it in extremely high regard and take it as proof positive that there was a Greater Intelligence at work, allowing themselves to be happy and elevated by the miracle.

CHAPTER HIGHLIGHTS

★ As human beings, we may be evolving to possess psychic and mediumistic abilities in response to our new, global family and increasingly wide-ranging and complex lifestyles.

★ Factual pieces of information, specific memories and clear mannerisms of the communicator in Spirit are compelling evidence.

★ Testing your mediumship under controlled conditions and recording your results is a great way to see how your practice could be improved and to build your confidence.

CHAPTER 7

UNIVERSE-ITY

I was thrilled to be invited by a psychic research group to speak at their conference about the Affirmation of Life.

My joy increased tenfold when I saw that I was to share the stage with one of my long-time heroes – Dr David Hamilton, bestselling Hay House author, scientist and teacher on the subject of the relationship between mind and body. I read my name next to his on the programme and smiled.

Dr Hamilton was speaking on the subject of compassion as a way to heal the heart, and I had been invited to share my thoughts about mediumship and give a demonstration of communication with Spirit. I named my talk 'Life After Life', and I was so excited to be making this presentation because I'm one of those freaks who loves, loves, *loves* public speaking, as well as being ever keen to do the work of Spirit, of course.

The day of the conference arrived and I spent some time welcoming the attendees, introducing myself and hobnobbing. The President of the psychic research group welcomed me and gave a generous and thoughtful presentation, then we left the stage for Dr Hamilton to open the day's talks.

He dazzled, as always, and soon it was my turn to take to the stage.

I'm going to tell you what I said in my talk later in this chapter, but for now, I'll skip ahead. I did my demonstration of mediumship and had a wonderful time. Although there were many sceptics in the room – the society's academics, scientists and research-minded members – I could tell by how the demonstration went that they were secretly believers. They gave me their full attention, their full energy and their full faith. I could feel it. And it showed in the quality of the communications that were able to come through me.

After my demonstration, I received a very welcome round of applause and I felt great. I made my way off the stage and lots of people came to say hello and share their thoughts and experiences about what we'd discussed. One particular person caught my eye: an elderly gentleman wearing two hearing aids and big spectacles, but with a lively and youthful energy about him. He was waiting patiently on the outskirts of the crowd to speak with me.

I spoke and spoke and spoke to people, then finally, it was his turn.

'That was extraordinary!' he declared. 'You have provided me with evidence beyond doubt that there are, somehow, mental entities... that perhaps *we*, each of us, are somehow mental entities that continue on after bodily death. Do you have a few minutes to answer some questions?'

Unfortunately, I didn't. I had talked and talked, and I was exhausted and starving hungry, having neither slept nor eaten the previous night because of anxiety about today's demonstration. So I smiled and politely bade him goodbye.

This all took place on the Saturday, and on Monday I was due back at university for the final year of my English Literature and Philosophy degree.

Monday arrived and I woke up much too late, still with the remnants of a Spirit hangover from Saturday's demonstration. My eyes sprang open and I quickly got dressed, scraped my hair back, brushed my teeth, smeared on a little make-up, pulled on my favourite worn-in leather boots and headed for the door.

It was a freezing cold day. I breathed dragon breath as I hoofed it up the steep hill upon which my lecture theatre was perched. I arrived at the door only to be greeted by a note saying that my lecturer was sick and someone else would be taking our consciousness class in a different building. And so I breathed and heaved some more and got myself to the correct room, just as fast as my late legs would carry me.

I hesitated for a moment, deliberating as to whether I should knock and make an entrance or try to slip in quietly and scuttle to my seat. I decided that the latter option was 99 per cent likely to be unsuccessful, so I knocked, swung open the door and smiled at my classmates who'd all turned around at the ruckus. Imagine my surprise when I looked up and locked eyes with a hearing-aided but sprightly gentleman who looked all too familiar.

My lecturer was the gentleman from Saturday!

I smiled and sat down, knowing my secret was out. I'd tried to hide my mediumship and psychic work from my peers at uni, uncertain as to how a school of analytic philosophers would react to my insistence on the continued existence of the human soul after bodily death, and unsure how to relate to people who *couldn't* relate to the seemingly absurd, yet life-affirming notion that was so precious to me.

But I knew I'd been outed. I could just tell. Something in the air made me feel super-conscious and hyper-aware that I'd recently been discussed.

I took my seat and the lecture continued as normal.

An hour later, I was eating lunch when I received an e-mail from another lecturer inviting me to her office to collect an essay. I went, and she opened the door, smiling. I sensed she wanted to say something, but didn't know how to say it. After a few minutes of chit-chat about the weather and my essay, she finally got to it.

'Professor Buchanan told me about your special ability. How long have you known you were a medium? My grandmother was a medium.'

I felt so confused and disoriented. I never expected to talk about my mediumship to anyone at university, or to have two professors in consciousness, science and analytic philosophy enquire about my experiences with open-mindedness, interest and sympathy. It felt weird. I didn't know if I'd wandered into the camp of a friend or foe. I wasn't sure whether to hug her and yell, 'Finally! Someone understands', or to hold back in case I was walking blindly into a sceptic's trap – the very thing I'd been protecting my mediumship against.

The Fear of Death in Disguise

Why had I been so afraid to speak my truth? Why had I been so reticent about my mediumship? I feared judgement because I felt that in being judged by my classmates, I'd be ostracized from the group. I worried that they would want to argue and debate my mediumship, and that I'd be forced to defend myself or, worse, that my confidence and faith in my work would be eroded. Behind all this lay a fear of losing my identity, my friendships and acceptance, along with a concern about bringing increased conflict and difficulties into my life. Behind this fear, in turn, was the fear that it would be painful, and that I'd be harmed. And behind this was the fear of death.

Try this self-exploration with your own fears. Whether you fear rejection, ridicule, being wrong, flying, spiders, speaking in public, ask yourself: what is behind this fear? When you examine that, ask: what is behind the fear that's behind the fear? Before long, you'll arrive at the conclusion: *I'm scared that I'll be harmed; I'm scared that I'll die.*

This experience at university was a very important one for me because in highlighting my fear of rejection, it highlighted the ways in which I was still afraid to die. And in so doing, it showed me the relationship between all other fears and the fear of death. This helped me to see the true power of excellent mediumship and of our loved ones in Spirit. When they come to us, or through us as mediums, they have the power to convince our recipients that they don't have to be afraid to die, and this can have a positive knock-on effect in healing their other fears as well. It was on the day I went to see my lecturer that I realized the true power and meaning of mediumship, and why our loved ones in Spirit come to us. It's not just about a message in a spiritualist church or a reading at a psychic fayre – it's about how we, and our recipients, apply those messages to who we are and how we live our lives. In giving recipients a compelling and true message from Spirit, we are asking them: how would you live your life if you did not have to be afraid? Which choices could you make if you could not be harmed? What would life be like if you started living from that place?

For many people, confirmation of life after death liberates them to speak more honestly, take bold chances, love again, go on wild adventures, apologize, forgive, spend more time with loved ones, seek the truth, start businesses, change harmful habits and ask for help. This is because they *know* they don't have to be afraid of being vulnerable, judged, rejected or scorned. They cannot die, and so they become free to truly live.

Wherever you are in your mediumship journey, please know that you carry immense power to help people in this way, and that what you're doing matters. Know that you yourself do not have to be afraid of rejection, ridicule, being wrong or any of the other fears that haunt us as mediums because you cannot be harmed – you cannot die. You are safe to love, speak boldly, make your way into people's hearts and minds and bring to light exactly what you find there. You are safe to be seen, to be visible and to speak the truth in love.

Mediumship in Space-time

I promised earlier that I would explain what I spoke about in my talk at the psychic research group. This might give you a handle on where you're getting the information from during your mediumship – something my students often tell me their rational minds get stuck on, causing them to overthink their work and become doubtful. Here is a condensed version of what I spoke about that day, and I hope that reading this will enable you to bypass that block and get on with the healing you're here to do.

The passage of time is one of the strangest and most mysterious elements of human experience. Philosophers have pondered, for thousands of years, the nature of time and our experience of it. Some schools of thought state that the past is fixed and the future is unknown, and that the only 'real' time is now – the present moment; other schools believe that the past and present are both fixed, but the future is not.

Our experience of time is largely dependent on the fact that humans have evolved to possess excellent faculties of causation and pattern recognition. So we have been able to make the movement of the planets *mean* that we are in a certain time, using this to create segments of the day, the representation of which, on a clock face, cause us to leave home for work, meet our friends or take the dog to the vet at a particular moment, rather than another.

Although it seems that much of time is constructed by the human mind, there is, nevertheless, something else in addition: a relationship between events, a feeling of moving from one moment to the next, a sense of progression – sometimes quickly, when we're doing something we enjoy, and sometimes slowly, when we're bored.

Contemporary research in science and philosophy suggests that moments and events that we call 'time' are not appearing and disappearing in a flash, as it might seem to our conscious awareness, but that all of time and space is happening simultaneously, for infinity, and it's the limitations of our individual experience of consciousness that are creating the sense – the illusion – that moments and events are flashing in and out of existence in a linear fashion. Yes, they *are* flashing in and out of awareness, but that doesn't mean that they flash in and out of existence. So where do they come from? And where do they go?

One answer is that space-time is vast, infinite and constantly in existence, and that waking human consciousness illuminates segments of it, one by one, moment to moment, like ascending floors on an elevator. Perhaps every event, every moment, every relationship is in its rightful place at all times, and we are just passengers on a ride, experiencing the dips, loops, crests and ascents that become available to our awareness.

What Does This Mean for Mediumship?

If space-time is four-dimensional, across three dimensions and expanded infinitely through the fourth, which is time, then that time your mother surprised you with exactly what you wanted for Christmas is happening right now, somewhere else in space-time. The day your beloved was born is happening right now, elsewhere. The very best moments of your life are playing out for eternity, and so are the most heartbreaking: your grandmother, your dad, your best friend, your aunt, your husband, your child – anyone you have ever lost is alive and well in the moments you cherish, elsewhere and elsewhen, amongst the Great Intelligence.

It is my belief that when I use my intuitive abilities – psychic or mediumship – I'm getting the information from other segments of space-time. And I'm able to access it by withdrawing from the sense of my own present moment. When I relax my mind and come away from the immediate moment, I allow my mind to be available to perceive other kinds of content besides the life and times of Lauren Robertson. At this point, you may think that all this seems very 'out-there', strange and unlikely, but just think of the clarity with which you can remember a significant memory. Now picture an apple in your mind, although there is no apple present, sing a song you know well, although there is no music – it is only one more step to perceive an event that you, as a medium, were not physically present for.

The Frontiers of Consciousness

I have dedicated this and the previous chapter to an explanation of why and how we have psychic abilities and mediumship, aligning it, as far as possible, with fact, science, philosophy and research and the state of the world as we know it. I have done this for a few reasons.

The first reason is, quite simply, because I find it fascinating – and I hope you do too! It is inspiring and exciting for me to question and explore the frontiers of consciousness and what the human mind can do. Another reason is that I want to draw a distinction between your psychic abilities and mediumship, which can be assessed, examined and considered within the framework of science and reality – and the more 'out-there' theories and interests in the mind, body and Spirit sector that don't lend themselves so well to research or evaluation. I hope you see that your abilities are a legitimate area for inquiry, study, research and development.

I also hope my theories are a source of courage and certainty about your mediumship – the more I have studied, researched and theorized around the topic of mediumship, the more confident I have become in my practice. One of the things I work on with my coaching clients is helping them to overcome self-doubt and the voices inside their heads that say, 'You can't do this', 'You're making this up' or, 'This kind of communication isn't possible'. I've found that having a logical and rational discussion about mediumship is an effective way to do this.

I hope that I've shown you that your mediumship *does* stand up to scrutiny and *does* fit within the world as we know it. And I hope that this will help you to treat your exploration of your own indelible Spirit with the enthusiasm of an intrepid adventurer, sparing you the hopelessness and demotivation that arise when you get that sinking feeling that you're 'making it all up' or 'kidding yourself'.

All That Being Said...

Your mediumship is sacred. You are sacred.

Treat yourself and your abilities as such. You will probably be excited to share your gifts, especially as you implement the techniques in this book and begin to experience new depths of healing and accuracy in your connection with Spirit, but you might want to exercise restraint in sharing your abilities, despite the urge to shout about them from the rooftops and talk about them with anyone who'll listen. In telling anyone and everyone, you risk exposing a beautiful and somewhat fragile flower to the elements. I recommend instead that you find yourself a supportive community, circle, group or organization whose principles, vibe and method you agree with, and where you feel safe, nurtured and supported – and in that space, feel free to let your mediumship bloom. Taking the flower analogy further, an orchid that is kept in a suitable greenhouse, at the correct temperature, in the right soil and given the appropriate amount of water, attention and care will blossom and thrive. An orchid that is left outside to face the elements – frost, wind, heat, etc.– will soon perish. Your mediumship is the orchid: find the right greenhouse and the very best conditions that will enable it to grow and flourish, especially when you're in the early stages of learning, with the support and community of like-minded people.

If you do choose to share your beliefs with family members, friends or colleagues who are unsympathetic, then not only do you become an annoying zealot, preaching to those who may not be interested, you also expose your mediumship to unwelcome criticism – the kind that erodes your confidence in your abilities. When someone you love and care for doesn't share a fundamental belief of yours, it can feel alienating and confusing. So go about your mediumship and personal growth with diligence and commitment, speaking of it only to sympathetic ears. Plug the energy drains created by arguing about it, and more power and energy will be redirected to your abilities.

It is not up to you to convince, cajole, coerce or in any way try to get others to understand or agree with you. Simply water and shelter your own orchid and let others deal with theirs in the way they see fit.

You will have noticed by now that my philosophy is that success in your mediumship is deeply dependent on your personal growth and development: as you grow, expand and reach ever higher levels of love, self-awareness and self-acceptance, your mind becomes freer and freer for Spirit to use. When you experience increased feelings of love, acceptance, happiness and peace, it will eventually become noticeable to those you care about, and so it is leading by example that will often influence your loved ones towards the cause of your positive change, in its own right time – like the orchid that blooms in exactly the right season.

I have created the following exercises to encourage you to focus on your successes, rather than your 'failures'. They are designed to help you turn away from the fear of death in all its forms, and instead to focus on how you and your mediumship have *given life* in your work, and how, in so doing, more life has been given to you.

In life, and in your mediumship, you get more of what you focus on. So if you want to trust yourself and trust Spirit more, and you want the information to come more consistently and with greater ease, then you must focus on the times when this has been true, instead of those when you didn't get it right or when you felt disappointed in yourself or your performance. Remember – you get what you focus on.

☆ ACTIVATION 15 ☆
A Journal of Your Successes

One simple strategy that helped me improve the quality of my mediumship was to keep a journal of my successes.

In addition to the one you've been using to do the work in this book so far, buy yourself a beautiful journal and dedicate it to recording the growth and development of your mediumship. This journal is to be used only to register your successes. As you advance with this practice, you may find yourself writing entire paragraphs or pages about the wonderful experiences you're having with your clients and recipients.

Mediumship training often teaches that we shouldn't be too proud of the things we get right, and that we should be humble and focus only on the areas we need to improve. Well, in my experience, both are important. To be human is to need feedback, encouragement, positive affirmation and markers of success.

You may be out of the habit of focusing on what you've done well, so I'm now inviting you to get back into it. When you're present, conscious, aware and thankful about the good you've created through your work with Spirit, you open yourself up for more of that good to come through you.

Be happy with even the smallest piece of evidence – it's OK to start small. Maybe you got the correct initial of someone in Spirit at a workshop? Maybe it was an improvement that you even raised your hand to participate in a workshop? Perhaps you perfectly embodied the mannerisms and posture of a mother in Spirit? Or perhaps a street name just 'arrived' with you in the middle of a reading?

The more you can be happy with the positive difference that evidence made to another person's life, the more frequent you'll find that these instances become. Spirit has no interest in your self-deprecation; Spirit wants you to thrive, succeed, be empowered and happy as a medium. So record instances when you worked well, so that you can readily access these feelings. Remember, you get more of what you focus on.

Keep your journal next to your bed, and every night you've worked with Spirit, write in it everything you're happy with, proud of, amazed and delighted by.

☆ ACTIVATION 16 ☆
Intention Setting in Your Mediumship

Imagine you set out on a journey, and you had a GPS in your car. Imagine you didn't know where you were going, and so you weren't able to input the address into your satnav. You'd be getting nowhere fast. And yet, when developing our mediumship, we rarely ever set goals or intentions. We focus on the next reading or the next workshop, without really setting an intention for what we want to get out of it, the kind of medium we want to be or in which ways we want to improve. And so we drive around with no destination in mind, not moving forwards at all. You can't get there if you don't know where 'there' is.

The following questions are designed to help you develop a meaningful destination in your mediumship – to help you set goals and intentions, so that you know where you want to go. Forming a clear idea of what you want to achieve is a powerful way to develop trust in yourself, in your mediumship and in Spirit. A destination gives you a marker of success to work towards, and the closer you get to this, the more certain you can be that your mediumship is effective, and your communication clear.

Turn to a clean page in your journal and write out the following questions, taking care to dig deep, be truthful and think big. Remember, Spirit wants you to succeed. Don't be ashamed of wanting to be an excellent medium and experience all that life has to offer along with it. When you have more, you create more for others.

- In a perfect world, what would your mediumship be like?

- How are you using it and what impact does it have?

- What qualities do you desire to embody as a medium?

- What is the next level of success for you in your mediumship?

- Where do you want your mediumship to be three months from now?

- What are your ultimate dreams/goals for your mediumship?

CHAPTER HIGHLIGHTS

★ **Find a supportive, nurturing community to grow your mediumship, and avoid discussing your abilities with anyone who might erode your confidence.**

★ **If all of space-time is happening at once, then all things are happening elsewhen and elsewhere. Perhaps you're accessing these moments in your mediumship.**

★ **Success leads to success: focusing on achievements in your mediumship encourages more of them.**

CHAPTER 8

GOOD VIBRATIONS

I was so frightened I could feel my heart beating in my ears. My fiancé had to shove me onto the bus, as I fought and resisted, begged and pleaded. I'd changed my mind. This was a stupid idea. I wasn't ready to get on that bus and face my greatest fear.

One week earlier, I'd broken into floods of tears – Alice-in-Wonderland-style sobs, during a one-to-one audience with a Buddhist lama whom I'd grown to love and trust. Tormented by powerful and constant feelings of shame, guilt and terror, the root cause of which I couldn't seem to put my finger on, I'd reached a point where I could no longer tolerate it, and had taken the opportunity to ask the one person who could not and would not judge me, if he could help me sort it out.

The tears had come when Lama Khemsar Rinpoche, barefoot, softly seated, gazed plainly, lightly and lovingly at me, and asked:

'When is the first time you recall having these feelings?'

As the words left his lips I was transported back to a moment I hadn't thought about in the longest time. I was eight years old. With too little pocket money to buy both a birthday card and present for my dad and a gift for my beloved gran whom I was visiting that day, I opted to buy a card for my dad and a box of chocolates for my gran. My intention was to visit Gran first and give her the chocolates, before making my way to my dad's house to give him his card, so he would be none the wiser.

I hadn't seen my dad much since he and my mum separated. But as I walked through the town, swinging the bag with my purchases as I went, who should walk around the corner but my dad, spotting me right away. He came over to say hello. We talked for a little while and his eyes kept looking down at the bag.

'Are they for me?' he asked as he moved to take the bag from my hand.

In my awkwardness and discomfort I yelled, 'No they're not for you!' – my anger, frustration and guilt at his leaving bubbling up, as I snatched the bag away from him and hid it behind my back. He moved his hand away, looking hurt and dejected, and although I was only eight, I remember feeling awful – like I'd wounded him, badly. My little body was wracked with guilt and shame. I felt nauseated and angry.

I didn't mean to hurt my dad's feelings, especially on his birthday. I wanted him to know that I loved him – that I cared.

I relayed all this to Lama Khemsar amidst pulsing tears and gut-wrenching sobs. He gazed at me with his transcendent look, utterly unfazed by the meltdown unfolding before him.

In his wisdom, he said nothing for what felt like ages; long enough for me to realize that I'd seen this pattern in my life again and again, and that I'd blamed my dad for everything: failed relationships, social anxiety, feeling unlovable, criticizing myself, never feeling content, being attracted to destructive men, having no idea how to 'be' in male company, being bad with money, loneliness, feeling misunderstood and every other painful experience I'd been involved in. According to me, it was all his fault for leaving, for starving me of love. This was the story I'd been telling myself since time immemorial – that I was doomed to make bad and unloving choices because my dad never loved me.

'So are the feelings of guilt and shame about you snatching a gift away from your father?' Lama Khemsar suggested with gentleness.

I nodded.

'And what did you get your father for his birthday this year?' he asked, innocently.

'Nothing,' I squeaked, as the waterworks started up again. Some new awareness was beginning to dawn on me as a result of Lama Khemsar's question, but I couldn't quite see it clearly yet. It was like looking through frosted glass.

'You have Buddha nature,' he stated. 'You have the ability to love, no matter what, so why are you choosing not to love your father?'

I inhaled, as if to give power and force to all the excuses and reasons that were about to spill out, but as I opened my mouth to speak, the penny suddenly dropped.

All these years, I'd thought the guilt and shame were because I had been unloved by my father and had made shameful choices as a result. But in that moment, everything changed. I understood, for the first time, that these feelings were not a result of him neglecting me; they stemmed from that day when I was eight years old, and every moment since, when I'd chosen not to love him.

I had chosen to be a distant, resentful and hateful daughter, when I had the chance to be loving, compassionate and understanding. And I'd been experiencing guilt and shame because I'd deserted my true self. I'd stopped being a source of light and warmth in this area of my life and had wandered off into the darkness instead. In that moment, I truly saw that I did love my dad, that I did desire to be a loving daughter to him and that I could easily picture myself being kind and loving towards him without needing anything back – without needing something that he, possibly, was not able to give me. I saw that I could light a candle of love for my dad from the flame of love that burns within me, illuminating many other areas of my life, and that doing so would never deplete me in any way – it would only add more light, more love to the world. I didn't need light from him to feel loved as I'd once thought. I was already lit. And perhaps it was he who needed love from me. I have Buddha nature. I am an infinite source of love and compassion. I am a light that can never go out. I can give my dad warmth and light. I can be generous, forgiving and open. I can be the daughter I always wanted to be. And I don't need him to change in order for me to do so.

All of this came to me in a split second, and I relayed my realization to Lama Khemsar.

'Freedom comes through action,' Lama Khemsar offered. 'To complete your healing and release yourself from shame and guilt you must take new actions – you must make that moment from when you were eight years old right again in your own mind. Buy your father a birthday present and take it to him.'

I blinked in disbelief and felt my heart begin to race. It was one thing to *apply* my Buddha nature; it was quite another to *do* Buddha nature. I hadn't seen or spoken to my father in 12 years.

'In Tibetan culture, white is the colour of purity, but through an action it is also associated with forgiveness. Buy him a white shirt for his birthday and deliver it by hand. Don't bother calling in advance, just turn up.'

… So there I was, sparkly gift bag and birthday card in hand (even though his 70th birthday was three months earlier) paralysed with fear and cold, shaking and too afraid to get on a bus to face my biggest fear: rejection from my father. Although I could see clearly that this fear was an illusion, and that my true pain was that I'd rejected myself in choosing to be angry and hateful, the illusion had built up massive power and energy, having been fed by me all these years. With gift in hand, Buddha in heart and no idea what to expect, I had to face him, hoping that it wasn't too late for me to make it right and be the compassionate daughter, woman, human being that I truly am. I had to apologize, let him off the hook and set myself free.

As the bus lurched, rocked and jolted out of Glasgow and towards where I grew up and my dad still lived, my heart raced harder and I trembled with fear.

All too soon, we reached the stop that would lead me to my dad's house. Weak-legged, I got off the bus and walked towards his home, everything in my body screaming at me to turn back, away from the danger of rejection.

Moments later, I approached his house, and a silence crept over me, like I'd finally acknowledged I was doing the right thing and had made peace with it. I felt Lama Khemsar beside me as I raised my hand to knock on the door. I swallowed hard and rapped lightly.

Silence.

Perhaps I'd knocked too gently.

I knocked again and rang the doorbell. Nothing.

Of all the possibilities, all the horrors of rejection, all the eventualities I'd played and replayed in my mind, him not being home had never been one of them.

I sat down on his porch with the gift bag next to me and exhaled, gathering my thoughts and going through the options of what to do next.

This was a silly idea, I thought. *I should head back towards town and get a soft drink at the pub, whilst I wait for the bus.*

I decided this was the best course of action and, defeated, made my way to the nearest pub. And, as I swung open the door, I immediately locked eyes with a familiar stranger: my father.

As long as I live I will never forget the look on his face.

He looked at me like I'd been at war – missing in action for so long that he'd given up hope, and now suddenly here I was alive and well, his beloved child. The look on his face told me everything I needed to know. It told me that I'd constructed a tragic and painful story about how my dad felt about me and that it was completely and utterly false. His expression pierced through the story instantly and it all came crashing down. He didn't hate me. He'd never hated me. He hadn't abandoned me. There was no malice or ill intent. There was no judgement of me as unlovable or unworthy; if anything, the only judgement I saw was the remnant of that he'd made on himself.

I gave him the gift purposefully, intentionally and consciously and apologized for missing his birthday all these years. We talked and talked for hours. He showed me that he had pictures of my sister and me on his phone, from when we were babies, and he was open, present and attentive. As I listened, learning more about this man who'd given life to me, I learned so much about myself too.

I cried all the way home, and the next morning, I was a new woman – a new medium.

Today, I am so grateful for this experience with my dad. Prior to our emotional meeting, I had no idea that the limiting beliefs I'd held about myself and my life could transfer themselves to my work with Spirit and cause me to be limited in my mediumship. Only when I was free of them did I see just how deeply they had held me captive, and just how powerful I could be as a woman, as a medium, once they were dismantled.

Liberation from Limitation

Following the realization that I'd made up a false story about my dad, I was shocked and amazed to find that the next time I gave a demonstration of mediumship, where once I had felt anxious, sick, fearful and unworthy of Spirit, I now felt calm, fulfilled, enthusiastic and happy during my precious work. I was no longer scared to say what was really there, or afraid of going for the detailed and emotional information. My mind had been freed from these prisons of thought, and Spirit began to work through me with increasing accuracy, power, healing impact and consistency. It was as if, in clearing out and releasing the debris of limiting beliefs, I'd created space for Spirit to speak. Finally, their whispers could be heard above the roar of self-criticism and self-rejection; because, in forgiving myself and my father, I'd left nothing more for my mind to shout about.

We all hold *plenty* of limiting beliefs about our mediumship, don't we?

- Do you believe you're not good enough?

- Do you feel disappointed in your mediumship?

- Do you believe that no one will pay you well for your work?

- Do you believe that Spirit has left you or taken your abilities away?

- Do you believe you've stopped growing as a medium?

- Do you believe you did a bad job with that last client?

- Do you believe you're not special enough?

- Are you afraid of public speaking?

- Do you beat yourself up after giving a message, and pick it to shreds?

What are the stories you're telling yourself that make these beliefs seem true? Where did the obsessive self-criticism and perpetual disappointment in your beautiful gifts come from? It might seem like it's about your mediumship, but it's not. A story – a web of limiting beliefs – was spun in your mind long ago, and this has imprinted itself on your mediumship, making such limited thinking about your work with Spirit seem right and true to you.

Resolving and healing the wound with my dad forced me to deal with the source of many fears, hesitations and doubts I'd been experiencing in my life: I feared judgement. I feared rejection. I doubted I was worthy. I doubted I was loved. I neglected myself. I feared not belonging. I feared I wasn't good enough. I didn't expect or ask for enough from my life. From the food in my fridge to funds in my bank account, I'd let things run down to zero, never being motivated to care for myself enough to replenish them until I'd gone hungry. I feared abandonment. I feared connection and trust. And each of these subtle, invisible and powerful ghosts dictated the way I lived my life … but what I never realized was that they were dictating my mediumship too.

Our Friend, the Ego

So if dropping limiting beliefs and negative stories is the key to freedom of information and expression in your mediumship, then who is the teller of these stories and how do we get that big-mouthed monkey to quieten down?

Well, the monkey, the storyteller, is your ego.

There is a lot of stigma around ego, and I often hear 'spiritual people' say that someone is 'full of ego', as if it's the worst thing you can be if you're a 'spiritual person'. But as a person of any sort, even a spiritual one, you need to accept the fact that you have an ego.

Ego is seen in many different ways, but for the purposes of this discussion, I am going to define it as *a conscious, thinking subject.*

Why Such a Bad Rap?

Your ego isn't the bad version of you. You needn't be afraid that by being yourself, talking about yourself positively, savouring things you enjoy or wanting the best for yourself, you're full of ego.

Your ego runs amok, causing you all kinds of pain and discomfort *only* when it has nothing constructive to consciously think about and is left to obsess over information, events and feelings – mostly negative ones, since it's caution that keeps us safe (caveman brains, remember?)

To demonize your ego in the context of your mediumship is a mistake because whatever you set up in your mind as an enemy, a block or a problem will become one simply because you believe it is.

If you give your ego a job to do, it quietens down. And in mediumship, your ego has a very important job to do. Its gift is in telling stories – it can help a communicator from Spirit to tell *their* story through you. So accepting that your ego is a friend and not an enemy can take your mediumship to the next level because, in doing so, you dismantle a powerful block.

Your ego is part of you and you are blessed. Your ego is enveloped by Spirit – it is part of Spirit, not outside of it. Your ego plays a necessary and important role in your mediumship. It is your sense of *self*; it is the capacity by which you, your recipient and the communicator in Spirit are individuated from each other, thus providing the necessary relationship for communication to take place. Without the ego there would be no mothers, fathers, daughters, sons, husbands, mediums, dogs or friends. Without ego, we would all be a nebulous blob of who-knows-what, with no sense of distinctness, identity or relationship with the world around us. Individuation and separation are the space in which love for one another is possible. *I* love *you*. Without individuation *I* and *you* would not exist and so the love that is between us could not exist either. The ego is Spirit's way of popping up in different forms and relating to itself in different ways – it's not the devil, and it's not something to hate yourself for and it's not a block to your mediumship. The problem with the ego arises when we don't understand or accept its function and value, and so it takes on the form of an unmanageable child that will not stop drawing on the walls, pulling things off shelves, covering the dog in nappy cream and switching the TV off whilst laughing at your rage. Your ego is no more your enemy than this child, and just like this child, if you give it a task to do, materials to draw with or something to expend its energy on, it's possible to look on lovingly as it does its work, with its tongue poking out the side of its mouth.

The Value of the Ego

You have probably been through some shocks, difficulties and trauma in your life – events that will have hurt you. It's part of being human. As a medium, these hurtful experiences are a blessing. The hard times you've been through give substance to your *phenomenological empathy (see pages 93–97)*. Communicators in Spirit can use the experiences that your ego has gone through to help explain their meaning more clearly, more compassionately and with greater accuracy. Plainly speaking, if you have been through divorce, abandonment, the death of a loved one, illness, abuse, redundancy, eviction or any other difficult life experience, then you are well equipped to pass on the message from a person in Spirit who has also gone through these things. You have an opportunity to bring additional clarity, emphasis and meaning to the subject you have in common with your communicator, leading to a powerful message that truly helps and heals.

But accessing your own difficult life experiences as a means to help Spirit express theirs is only possible if you yourself have healed from the trauma of your own past. If you are still caught up in the pain, then you will be unable to bring the necessary distance, spaciousness and objectivity to the communication, leading to messages that are a mixture of Spirit's message and your own anguish.

When I was 21, I was hospitalized for three weeks, followed by a three-month recovery at home as a result of viral meningitis. Now, if there's a person in Spirit who also had meningitis, I'm able to go there with them because I understand, and because I've healed the fear and pain that arose from this experience, such that I can talk about it somewhat objectively. Contracting meningitis was the beginning of a significant healing journey for me in which I learned that by caring for myself, inside and out, I was further empowering myself to be a vessel for Spirit, for their Truth. So whenever something challenging happens in my life, I'm always immediately grateful for it (even if it hurts) because I know that it's happening for me, so that I can help someone in Spirit with this very same situation in future. That knowledge brings healing in itself. None of this would be possible without my ego, my sense of being a conscious, thinking subject: my identity as Lauren Robertson.

☆ Activation 17 ☆

Acknowledging and Transcending Limiting Beliefs

We all carry with us beliefs about our limitations. Mediumship is such a special, subtle and profound gift that it often triggers many self-criticisms, fears, doubts and old conditionings that tells us why we can't do it. A lot of mine were to do with my dad and feeling that I was unloved, and they manifested in all sorts of different ways in my mediumship:

- I believed my clients were judging me.

- I believed my clients were criticizing me.

- I believed I wasn't good enough and my recipient wouldn't be happy with what I told them.

- I believed I'd never be well paid as a medium.

- I worried that I was going to get it wrong.

- I feared that I'd hurt my clients' feelings unintentionally.

Each of these beliefs was rooted in my quest for my dad's love and approval, but all they served to do was staunch the miraculous, infinite, loving flow of my mediumship.

This exercise will help you to make way for new, supportive and encouraging beliefs, by dispensing with the old. Here's what you need to do:

In your journal, write out all the ways in which you criticize your mediumship, and yourself as a medium. Write out all the negative thoughts, fears, doubts and frustrations – especially those that go around and around in your head like a broken record. Now pick one – the one that seems most painful, most frequent, most limiting, most annoying.

Got it?

Now with this belief in mind, write down your answers to the following questions:

- In what other areas of your life are you making a similar criticism of yourself?

- When was the earliest time in your life you remember feeling this way or hearing this criticism about yourself? (Think back to childhood.)

- Who told you that this is your place in the world and this is the way the world is?

- Whose voice was the first to make this criticism?

- Whose love did you crave most as a child – your mother's or your father's?

- Who did you have to be to gain your mother's/father's approval and love?

- In what way are you treating Spirit or your recipients as if they are your mother/father?

- What is your mother's/father's story? How were they treated when they were young?

- If you could be an adult, and see your parents as children, what would you say to them?

- If you could return to one moment and speak to yourself as a child, what would you say to little you?

- What do you want to be true about your mediumship?

- Are you available to stop being the child and treating Spirit/your recipients like your parents?

- If not the child, who are you going to be instead?

- What will you believe instead?

- What will you say to yourself about your mediumship instead?

- What will change in how you show up as a medium?

- What do you feel now?

This line of enquiry takes you on a journey of why you think the way you do, who taught you to think that way and how you can change it. Often, our doubts, fears and self-critical beliefs are given to us by our parents, but if you can't find the root of the limiting belief in this line of questioning, try replacing your mother/father story with your siblings, grandparents or teachers – whoever was influencing you from the age of seven or younger.

☆ Activation 18 ☆
Knowing, Growing, Showing

Great mediumship is a collaboration between you and Spirit, and the better you know yourself, your talents and your interests, truly seeing them as strengths and sources of information that Spirit can use, the more accurate your mediumship will become. You don't have to reach for some far-out galactic message; the best messages you give from Spirit will be those that are most human, and those of which you have intimate knowledge, because you are most confident in handling that kind of information. For example, a nurse who is familiar with the names of various illnesses and the process of dying in a hospital is well equipped to receive specific details about a person in Spirit's illness and death; a medium with an encyclopaedic knowledge of music can confidently share songs that were important to the communicator, and describe musicians, singers and songs from Spirit with great ease and assurance.

One of the finest mental mediums who ever lived was Albert Best, and he was able to tell his recipients the full name, address and postcode of the communicator from Spirit because he'd been a postman!

The most spectacular information from Spirit often comes from connecting with what is most *human* about the communicator. If you have a communicator from Spirit who shared the same hobby as you, who has a name that's familiar to you or who experienced life and its twists and turns similarly to you, then you will have a stronger resonance with these people in Spirit – just as happens in life.

So if you want to improve at bringing specific details through from Spirit, think about the specifics of life you're already confident talking about, then expand your knowledge in that area – give yourself the language, the words, the vocabulary – place it in your mind, and Spirit will use it. Work with this idea and you'll be able to convey certain messages with greater confidence, ease and insight.

This is especially true of names, street names, hobbies and interests, medical terminology or careers. The more you expand your knowledge and awareness, the more easily Spirit can use this to communicate their meaning.

Answer the following questions, and create a plan for developing your confidence in receiving and conveying specific details from Spirit:

- What specific details do I want to make available for Spirit to use?

- What do I need to do to put more of that kind of information into my mind?

- What do I need to do to become more confident in talking about this kind of information?

CHAPTER HIGHLIGHTS

★ The limiting beliefs you hold about yourself and your life can transfer themselves to your mediumship, causing you to become limited in your work with Spirit.

★ Your ego is not the enemy. The ego's gift is in telling stories, and yours can help your communicator tell their story through you.

★ Spirit will often access your life experiences to help you explain their meaning – *if* you have healed your pain in that area.

CHAPTER 9
ENVY AND BELIEF

A *re you serious? He's got 20,000 Facebook followers? I*
thought, catching a glimpse of my bespectacled face in
the computer screen, made ugly and contorted by jealousy
and scorn.

He was a new, young medium – an excellent medium
– who'd exploded onto the scene and immediately become
a sensation. He could bring through anyone from Spirit and
identify them by their first name and surname: the holy grail
of evidential mediumship.

I was due to demonstrate mediumship at a local spiritualist
church that evening, and had spent all day cyber-stalking
him – looking at all his sold-out dates and glossy website,
which was unlike anything I'd managed to create for myself.
I had been thrown into a state of rage and confusion – the
whole situation bringing up the deepest conflicts of my inner
self.

On one hand, I was thrilled that he was doing the work
of Spirit so amazingly well, demonstrating beyond doubt that
we remain connected to the people we love after we/they die.

But the human part of me who'd soldiered on and turned up to spiritualist churches, often paying for the pleasure of doing so, to demonstrate mediumship for four people, was jealous and disappointed. In fact, I was seething with jealousy.

I was jealous of his ability to be at one with Spirit so effortlessly when I'd been grinding away at it for years. I was jealous that I'd received minimal support as a young medium and he had the world flocking around him to help him get to the top. I was jealous that he could assist miraculous transformation in people's lives by uttering two words. I was jealous that his events sold out from day one. I was jealous that he had marketing, promotion, PR and event teams, which allowed him to focus on being a medium of excellence. And I was jealous that he was so brilliant – because it was as brilliant as I wanted to be.

I desperately wanted to know his secret. Twelve months earlier, this person didn't even know he was a medium. Now he was one of the best in the world.

I thought I might as well stop doing mediumship if I couldn't be as good as him – it clearly wasn't my zone of genius as it seemed to be his. Yet, I knew I'd helped people immeasurably, and that Spirit communication was in my warm breath, under my fingernails, between the tiny hairs on the back of my neck and in the deepest recesses of my mind, like being perpetually, madly, in love. There was no way I could separate myself from it.

So why did Spirit find him deserving of such a gift and not me, after the commitment and dedication I'd shown? I was so effing jealous I could almost feel myself turning green. But Spirit works in mysterious ways, and I knew there had to be a blessing in my envy if I was willing to see it.

I dragged myself away from the computer and went to my room to do a meditation. I thumped myself down on my pillow like a petulant child and closed my eyes. I breathed deeply and felt the inspiration travel through my entire body. I breathed and I breathed, moving farther and farther away from my bedroom with each breath.

Thank him and bless him for showing you it can be done.

And suddenly I understood. My eyes darted open – the caffeine-like effect of true inspiration.

'He's showing me it can be done,' I whispered aloud.

I closed my eyes once more and visualized myself with the qualities I so admired in him. I visualized myself speaking graciously, openly and unselfconsciously – allowing the truth of people in Spirit to be spoken through me. I visualized their first names and surnames leaving my mouth clearly and naturally, as if I was introducing people I knew well.

I smiled, knowing that anything a woman's mind can believe, it can achieve.

That evening, I arrived at the spiritualist church and sat in the medium's room. I took myself back to my visualization and said in my mind: I know you want to share everything with me that would prove you're still here. I know it's only me that's holding back. Please help me be who and what I need to be to say your first name and surname correctly.

When it was time, I approached the platform. I was called to do the opening prayer, so I made my way to the front of the platform, bowed my head and began.

It's George Campbell, I heard, as clear as if he was standing next to me. I was even more thrilled when a single hand went up amongst the packed audience, belonging to someone who did, indeed, know George Campbell in Spirit.

George was the first communicator who identified himself by first and surname (thank you, George) and there have been many more since.

I was amazed and thrilled at being able to give this calibre of evidence, and having discovered what it took to do it once, I knew what was required of me if I wanted it to happen again.

In hindsight, I am grateful for my experience of envy because it taught me an important lesson that vastly improved the quality of my mediumship. I finally became convinced that my connection with Spirit was limited only because I believed that it was; by changing my beliefs about my mediumship, I changed my mediumship.

The Law of Attraction

In your mediumship, replacing unsupportive thoughts and beliefs with loving and supportive ones is about more than just changing your state of mind so you feel better. There is a spiritual philosophy known as *the Law of Attraction*, which is based on the idea that changing your state of mind changes your reality by attracting to you experiences that are in alignment with your thoughts, beliefs and emotions.

This may sound magical or spooky, but it's actually very logical. Your thoughts and beliefs cause you to feel a certain way. Those feelings, in turn, motivate you to take certain actions and those actions create a certain reality. For example, if you want to visit Florence, Italy this year, you begin by thinking of Florence. When you think of Florence, you feel a certain way. That feeling motivates you to book your flights, look at nice hotels, save money to spend, pack your case and turn up at the airport. So the result of your thoughts, feelings and actions is that you experience the reality of waking up in Florence.

There are many people, however, who want to go to Florence who never do. Why is that? This is where the Law of Attraction gets tricky. Many of the thoughts, beliefs and emotions that create our reality are subconscious. They were given to us in our early years and have been running on auto-pilot ever since – and not all of them are good. Someone who really wants to go to Florence might have the subconscious belief that they don't deserve the trip, that it's a waste of money, they haven't earned it, etc. So instead, they procrastinate.

It's like the example I shared with you earlier in the chapter. I really wanted to be able to receive first names and surnames, but I believed I couldn't. I believed I had to work hard to earn my gifts as a medium. I believed I wasn't good enough to receive names. So although I really wanted to, these other emotional beliefs were countering my desire, causing me to experience the reality of not being able to receive names.

And there is one other tricky thing about the Law of Attraction. It can be difficult to change your thoughts, feelings and emotions, *and* to sustain that change for long enough to see different results in your reality. When your reality appears a certain way, it justifies the thoughts that created it, and not necessarily the new thoughts you're trying to focus on – the ones that will create your new reality. Your mind is always trying to match your inner world to your outer reality, so you have a better chance of surviving and thriving because you are reacting accurately to the world and that way you stay safe. When you try to *change* your beliefs, it can feel difficult and uncomfortable as your mind struggles between your new beliefs and the 'reality' that's right in front of you.

One of my ambitions is to be hotter, happier and healthier in my 30s than I was in my 20s. In order to accomplish this, one of the things I do is to work out at a boxing gym. But already I have missed sessions, opting to lie on the couch instead, even though I really want to go. Why? Because my reality – the reality of lying on the couch, watching TV – is what I'm accustomed to; and at only three weeks into my new gym routine, I haven't yet seen results, so the temptation to do what I've always done instead is strong. The Law of Attraction cannot fail – you are always attracting *something*. Failure to change our reality is usually due to our inability to sustain our new thoughts and feelings until we see *results*. You are always thinking thoughts, and you are acting on your beliefs (some of them subconscious). As long as this is so, you are constantly attracting circumstances that are in-line with those thoughts and beliefs.

Working with the Law in Your Mediumship

In the context of your mediumship, have you ever thought any of the following:

- *I'm not good enough.*

- *My recipient wasn't happy with what I told her.*

- *My mediumship is rubbish.*

- *I'll never be as good as…*

- *I'm not getting anything.*

- *I feel ridiculous.*

- *I can't do this.*

- *I'm talking nonsense.*

- *Spirit doesn't exist.*

- *I couldn't do platform.*

- *My gifts have closed down...*

... or any number of other thoughts that make you feel horrible.

How do these thoughts make you feel? Are they causing you to create the reality you want in your mediumship?

Now, let's consider the outcomes we *do* want to attract into our mediumship: happy recipients, accurate and detailed information, joyful and compelling communication; wonderful opportunities to do our work, feeling fulfilled and energized, effortless impact and healing, miraculous conversations, dream clients – and whatever else you want from your communion with Spirit. What are the thoughts and beliefs that would need to be true for you to draw these outcomes to you? How will it feel when you achieve them? Imagine you're sailing in a beautiful boat down the river of Spirit, and you're headed for a wonderful destination. You want to get there as fast as you can, and you depend upon the Divine winds picking up and filling your sails, propelling you forwards. Imagine, too, that the Divine winds are raised by your positive thoughts – the ones that are light and loving, which lift you up and elevate you. We want more of these please; we want your little ship moving towards its destination, carried confidently on the river of Spirit, its sails full of elation.

Here are some of those thoughts:

- *I'm grateful I was able to play my part as medium in helping this person.*

- *My mediumship is a blessing in my life and the lives of others.*

- *I appreciate my connection with Spirit.*

- *I am a powerful medium.*

- *I am loved.*

- *It is safe for me to be powerful, direct, clear and confident.*

- *I am worthy of my abilities and the task of sacred communication.*

- *I work with great accuracy, compassion and sensitivity.*

- *My recipients are thrilled with the messages I deliver.*

- *I love and appreciate myself.*

- *My best is good enough and everything is working out perfectly.*

- *I can easily receive names and other specific details from Spirit.*

Every time you think a supportive, loving thought about yourself and your mediumship, you get a little wind in your sails and the thought becomes movement, action, towards your destination. This is the Law of Attraction as I see it. Just notice how different your body feels, as you say these sentences in your mind or out loud (hint: that's a good idea at this point – go back and say them out loud), compared to the earlier set of limiting statements.

To begin this commitment to selecting your thoughts often requires regular examination: is what you are thinking true? Should you accept the thought? Is it supportive or limiting?

Should you keep or transform it? Conscious examination of your beliefs along these lines and perpetual judgement of whether and how they are serving you is a healthy lifelong habit that will get you closer to the results you seek, as long as you keep practising.

The Mind–World–Mind Cycle

So we've identified the difference between limiting and supportive thoughts and beliefs, and we're clear on the ability of our thoughts to attract or create an equivalent event in the world. But what can we do to harness and apply this principle to help us in our mediumship?

There are four 'entry points' in the mind–world–mind cycle of the Law of Attraction and we can create elevation in any one of them in order to begin attracting the results we want in our mediumship. The entry points are: feelings, beliefs, words and actions.

There are a variety of techniques you can use to influence either your feelings, thoughts, words or actions to start a cycle of justification that attracts the reality of what you *do* want to you. When you work with any one element, the others in the cycle are positively affected, and just as your mediumship is transformed for the better, your confidence and experience of life will be too because the beliefs you hold about your mediumship are a reflection of the beliefs you hold about other things.

The key to using the Law of Attraction to improve your mediumship is to become intimately aware of *how you want to feel*: cultivate the emotional experience of what you do want, rather than indulging in worry and fear about what

NEGATIVE

Justification for the thought is sought and found.

Emotional thought: *'My mediumship is not good enough.'*

Mind

Underlying thought: *'I'm not good enough.'*

World

Actions and behaviour occur in line with the thoughts, and the beliefs grow stronger.

POSITIVE

Justification for the thought is sought and found.

Emotional thought: *'My mediumship truly helps people.'*

Mind

Underlying belief: *'I am worthy and valuable.'*

World

Actions and behaviour occur in line with the thought.

you don't want, and the magnetic power of your positive emotions will call the experience towards you from the Great Intelligence. The point is to transcend the compulsion to focus on the emotions you don't want – the painful, negative emotions associated with limiting thoughts – and train your mind to savour the strong, positive emotions linked with what you do want. The energy of the positive emotion is what pulls it to you in reality, so the aim is to get you feeling as great as possible about your work with Spirit, and the positive results will follow.

For many of my students and clients, this is a key piece of work we do together that gives them freedom and takes their mediumship to a whole new level. For a medium who's spent their whole life believing that they're not good enough, to begin to see themselves as worthy, capable and loved in the eyes of Spirit, can be transformational – not just for them, but for the Spirit communicators and living recipients they'll go on to serve with greater confidence, conviction and compassion.

Here are some approaches we can use to transform a negative cycle of justification into a positive one:

- We transform our emotions by managing our thoughts.

- We transform our emotions by examining our beliefs.

- We transform our emotions by embracing our desires.

- We transform our emotions by selecting our words.

- We transform our emotions by directing our actions.

And read on, because in the Activation section of this chapter, I'm going to help you to do just that.

☆ ACTIVATION 19 ☆
Feeling

If we want to create a certain emotion or feeling in our mediumship, to motivate us to take bold new actions, we first have to identify which feelings we want to experience. When I'm working with Spirit, I want to feel elation, enthusiasm, peace, steadiness and love. Now it's your turn: answer the following two questions to gain clarity in how you want to *feel*. (If you're struggling to find the right feeling, or the right words to describe what you want to feel, I recommend searching online for 'wheel of emotions' and spending some time with a thesaurus.) Go with your gut and choose whichever words feel right to you with this one.

1. How do you want to feel when practising your mediumship?

2. What are you going to do now in your life to feel the way you want to feel?

☆ ACTIVATION 20 ☆
Believing and Thinking

When transforming your thoughts and beliefs about yourself and your mediumship, it can be helpful to model the qualities and behaviour of someone you think a lot of. The following exercise is designed to help you identify the qualities you admire in others. This is a first step towards integrating them into yourself, either by acknowledging that you already have them or by gaining clarity on what you'd like to emulate moving forwards.

- Write down in your journal the name of a medium, spiritual practitioner, famous person or someone you love and hold in high regard.

- Now write out 10 things you admire about them.

- Do this again for someone else you look up to. Notice if there's any crossover or qualities that have come up repeatedly.

- Now write down your own name.

- In which ways have you already shown that *you* have these qualities – in your life and in your mediumship?

- What are you going to do, moving forwards, to embody those qualities?

☆ ACTIVATION 21 ☆
Speaking and Writing

Words are powerful. When we're consciously creating a certain reality in our mediumship, it's important that we focus on speaking and writing words that move us closer to our goal, and avoid those that might undermine our transformation, and set us back. You may have heard of 'positive affirmations'. These are intentional statements about the positive things we want to be true. There are three powerful ways to work affirmations:

1. Think, write or speak a new belief repeatedly to help your mind absorb it.

2. Use your affirmation as an 'anchor'. Make it your online password, the screensaver on your phone or a note on your fridge, so that you anchor it into your day.

3. Use it as a 'pattern interrupter'. If you catch yourself in a negative spin, say 'No!' and use your affirmation to direct your mind to more positive thoughts.

Affirmations traditionally begin 'I am...' – so what are you? What do you want to be true about yourself as a medium? (Helpful hint: stay away from 'not', and 'don't' – for example, 'I am a medium who doesn't feel fear – as these affirm what you don't want. Instead, focus on affirming what you *do* want – for example, 'I am a brave and courageous medium'.) My favourite is: 'I am a calm, confident and compassionate medium.'

Now you: what do you want to be true about your mediumship? Start with, 'I am...'

☆ ACTIVATION 22 ☆
Action

Action is the key to your success as a medium. If you are taking consistent, bold actions towards your desired outcome, sooner or later you must meet with success. It's just a case of simple maths that a medium sitting in a great circle twice a week, sitting in the power every day and giving 20 messages a week, come rain or shine, is going to be further along than one who does a practice reading once a month. Often, there's something we're doing – or not doing – that prevents us from seeing the results we desire. The questions in this section will help you to identify whether you need to be taking different or more consistent actions.

- What have you been doing that's creating the results you're currently experiencing in your mediumship?

- What have you been neglecting to do that's causing the results you're currently getting?

- What are you going to do differently to achieve the results you desire in your mediumship?

- What are you going to stop doing to enable you to achieve the results you desire?

☆ ACTIVATION 23 ☆
Vision Board

Creating a vision board for my mediumship has helped me to remain focused on what I want and kept me motivated towards creating the joyful, abundant and miraculous connection with Spirit I desire. I also think that having a vision board around is a way to bring the energy of what you want into the present constantly and automatically, whilst you're off doing other things.

A vision board is simply a board (physical or electronic) incorporating depictions of each of your desires. Mine is a large cork board that stands on my dressing table, so it's the first thing I see in the morning and the last thing I see before going to sleep. On it are the following: a smiling audience – because I desire to uplift many people with mediumship; a stack of books – because I want to write a stack of books about mediumship (it's happening – yay!); a blonde woman in meditation with a blossoming rose on her heart – because I desire to be compassionate, passionate, loving and caring in my mediumship; several pairs of Manolo Blahnik shoes – because a girl's gotta be well shod for Spirit!; and a number of other things that depict the kind of medium I want to be and the role I want my practice to play in my life and the lives of others.

Now it's your turn. I want you to create a vision board with images, cut-outs, printouts, etc. – anything that represents the kind of medium you want to be, how you see yourself serving others with your gifts and the role this work will play in your life.

Helpful hint: Spirit does not judge your desires. If you want to earn a living in exchange for your mediumship, put this on your vision board. If you want to speak in front of large audiences, use an image to represent this. It's important that the images you select are emotionally charged and things that you really, really want and care about. Remember, it's the emotion that motivates you and causes you to make the often subtle changes that create your desired reality.

Have fun with this and enjoy bringing the energy of your dreams and desires visually into the present. And remember: Spirit is watching, listening and working, and is keen to give you what you want.

CHAPTER HIGHLIGHTS

★ Each time you work with Spirit, you have a say in how accurate, impactful and successful the communication can be via the beliefs and thoughts you choose.

★ You can manifest accuracy, confidence and excellence in your work with Spirit by engaging with the Law of Attraction, using the same techniques you would to receive money, a new relationship or a new home.

★ The key to manifesting amazing results in your mediumship is to focus on how you want to feel and practise cultivating the emotional experience of what you *do* want, instead of indulging in worry and fear about what you *don't* want.

CHAPTER 10
THE POWER OF 'NO'

M y doorbell rang.

I opened the door, and there stood a beautiful, elegant, neatly dressed woman in her 50s. She'd won a one-to-one reading with me in a raffle at a charity ball, and she was here to collect her prize. I smiled warmly at her and welcomed her into my home. I made sure she was comfortable, offered her some water and talked her through what was about to happen in her reading, confirming with her that she understood and was happy with how we were going to proceed.

I began recording our session on my phone, closed my eyes for a moment and settled into her presence, optimistic that the session would go well. After a short time, I started speaking.

'I get the sense that you've come here today with many questions and that you've been feeling frustrated and confused about several different matters in your life. Is that correct?'

'Yes,' she replied.

… and that, dear reader, was pretty much the first and last 'Yes' I heard from her during the entire session. No matter how hard I tried, how clear the people in Spirit seemed to me or how specific I endeavoured to be, I kept getting the same response: 'No.'

'Do you know this kind of person in Spirit?'

'No, I don't think so.'

My face glowed with embarrassment.

'Does this street name mean anything to you?'

'Not that I can recall.'

I took a deep breath, trying not to sound exasperated.

'Do you remember when this, this and this happened?'

'No, I'm afraid I don't remember that.'

My mouth and throat became dry as I realized this was not going well. And so we went, grinding away at it, unable to see eye to eye over anything. I was exhausted, and she seemed both disappointed and bamboozled.

At the end of the reading I clicked off the recording. 'I know there were lots of things you said "No" to throughout the reading,' I said. 'Give it a little time, perhaps; listen to the recording and, hopefully, some of it will begin to make sense… Just as well you didn't pay for this reading or I'd have offered you your money back,' I joked, as us Scots are known to do as a means to relieve awkwardness.

She left and I flopped down on the couch, placed a cushion over my face and screamed. I was confused, exhausted and disappointed. But mostly, I was frustrated – frustrated that the reading had gone so horribly wrong, and that because I didn't know why, there was nothing I could do about it. After a few minutes, I managed to pull myself together and get over the drama. I knew there was something the woman had needed, and that I had been unable to give it to her. I closed my eyes and prayed for her: *Dear God, please help her, guide her, envelop her in love and ensure that what she needs to see is revealed to her. Amen.*

There was nothing more to do after that, but forget about it and get on with my life.

Three months later…

'Hello. I'd like to see you for a reading. Today, if possible. Are you available?'

A woman's voice – calm, well-spoken, riding a wave of excitement and urgency – was on the other end of the phone.

I looked at my watch.

'Yes, I can see you today. Does 2 p.m. work for you?'

'Yes, 2 p.m. is perfect.'

I started to give her my address, but was interrupted.

'I know where you live,' she said. 'I'll see you then.'

She hung up and I had no idea what to expect. I surmised that she must be a previous client if she knew my address, but of all the people I expected to see when I opened the door, the neat and tidy woman whose reading had gone horribly wrong three months previously was not one of them. And yet there she stood.

She came in, gracefully removed her expensive coat and neatly folded it over the back of her chair. I swallowed hard, dreading a repeat of my previous performance.

'Before you do my reading, I'd like to tell you something,' she began.

'Sure – shall we sit down?' I offered.

'I don't know if you remember but I came to you for a reading a few months ago, after winning a session with you in a raffle. Anyway, there were some things you said about my family who've passed on now that I couldn't verify because I'm actually adopted.'

Lord! How could I have missed that? I thought. 'Go on,' I said.

'I just wanted to let you know that I have been searching for my birth mother for 40 years, and I've had no luck at all. No leads, no news, no contact – absolutely nothing. And for 40 years I've felt empty, unloved, worthless and like I'm living half of a life, with no identity because I don't know who I am or where I came from.' She looked down solemnly at her hands and paused, as if to gather her feelings.

'I wanted to come here and thank you for the audio recording of my reading last time. I listened to it and you passed on a piece of information from my dad, who you alleged had passed. It didn't mean anything to me in the moment, but so desperate was I to find my birth family that I followed it up thinking that anything was worth a try.'

She looked up at me and straight into my soul, her eyes brimming with tears.

'And, well, I just wanted to let you know that the piece of information you gave me from Dad turned out to be correct. It led directly to my birth mother. I found her – we found each other, after all this time. My lifelong search is over. We'll be spending our first Christmas together this year. She was as broken-hearted about losing me as I was about losing her. We can both heal from our separation now. I feel like a new woman, like a different person – thank you, and thanks, Dad.'

She smiled and looked Heavenward.

I could feel myself becoming choked up as a hurricane of emotions stirred up inside me. I was filled with the deepest humility. It felt like I was breathing in true love. In that moment, it felt like I could have dropped dead and been happy, knowing that I'd truly helped someone – knowing that I'd witnessed a miracle. I felt more filled up with Spirit than ever before, like my life had real meaning. It was as if some Higher Power had brought us together and was crying tears of joy with us.

She looked at me, bright-eyed and childlike, and we hugged and sobbed together. Then, with her dainty hands, she picked up her coat, smoothed down her skirt and we said goodbye as people normally would.

But we were, each of us, changed for ever.

I never saw her again, but on days when it's raining a bit too hard, or when my hair won't sit right, or I'm running late or getting furious about having to clean the toilet, I think of her dad in Heaven, and of her eating Christmas dinner together with her mum for the first time – and I laugh.

The Meaning of 'No'

The word 'no' is kryptonite to mediums. When a recipient says 'no' to a piece of information we pass on from Spirit, we can feel anything from a light flutter of embarrassment to wanting the ground to swallow us up. But the moral of the story I've just told is that when you hear the word 'no' from your recipient, you have a choice: you can get all caught up in the drama and conclude that you're a bad medium, that you couldn't help your client, that you should stop doing this work and that you ought to be embarrassed (as I did); *or* you can choose to make it mean something else. If we choose to use it in the right way, the word 'no' can actually help us improve our mediumship. So I'm going to devote the remainder of this chapter to exploring the power of 'no'.

Taking control of our relationship to the word 'no' – mastering the art of getting it wrong – can be one of the most powerful ways to elevate the quality, consistency and healing impact of your mediumship. As we've discussed in previous chapters, many of the fears that pop up in our mediumship have their roots in our early life experiences, and our fear of the word 'no' is no exception: the strength of your reaction to it when it's said by your client is generally a reflection of your fear around it in other past contexts.

When a recipient says no to a piece of information, what are they really saying? They're simply saying that it doesn't ring true for them right now. But we tend to think that they're saying: *you're wrong*. We make it mean something about *us*, and that's where the pain gets triggered. On a subconscious level, their 'no' might remind us of feeling abandoned by our mother, being made a fool of in class when we didn't know the answer, being rejected by our siblings, our parents having no money to buy us nice things or feeling worthless and ignored. These are the connections our minds make when a client says 'no', because our brains are wired to avoid rejection – and this is where the pain and embarrassment come from when they do so.

The Gift of 'No'

The beauty of being human is that once we see that we are acting out a certain belief – once we become conscious of it – we then have the option to change it. I'm now going to invite you to decide whether you'd like to continue being hurt by the word 'no' or begin seeing it as a blessing in the development of your mediumship because it shows you where there is still room to grow in your work with Spirit. Just as Edison had to find 9,999 ways in which the light bulb didn't work before he arrived at the one that *did*, so must we treat a 'no' as an opportunity to grow, try again and get it right next time.

Earlier we looked at the importance of applying critical thinking and experimentation to your mediumship, and never was it more appropriate to do so than when examining why a client said 'no' to a piece of information. Rather than thinking that the 'no' is about you and reacting, as a result, with emotion, try to investigate the reason for it and work to adapt your communication with Spirit accordingly – then you will find that 'no' was the greatest gift your recipient could have given you. This is especially so if you are still practising and learning as a student. I recommend that you try to collect as many 'no's as possible with your friends and circle members, and I'll explain further why this is important and how to go about it in the Activation section of this chapter. Before that, however, I'd like to discuss some of the most common reasons why recipients have said 'no' in my experience.

Your Recipient Doesn't Understand What You Mean

Language is complicated. Even the simplest of sentences can be misunderstood. You need only think about a time when you've misjudged the tone of an e-mail to see how rapidly understanding can be lost. If you think your recipient has said 'no' because they don't understand what you mean, try breaking the piece of information down into smaller pieces or saying it in a different way. Be clear, specific and concise with your communication to minimize the occurrence of this type of 'no'.

Your Recipient Doesn't Use the Same Style of Language as You

We discussed that our mediumship is a reflection of our dominant sense – the one we use to describe the world (*see pages 54–57*). If you are portraying your recipient's loved one differently from how they would, it can seem that the two of you are speaking two different languages (sometimes you really *are* speaking two different languages, in the case of international recipients). So, again, making sure the language you use is simple and clear, whilst remaining true to the communicator, and asking the recipient for a 'yes' or a 'no' after every piece of information can help to resolve this kind of misunderstanding.

You've Given Too Many Pieces of Information to Your Recipient

Did you express a complex idea or get caught up in the narrative and let several pieces of information come out at once? If so, it may have been a 'yes' for some and a 'no' for others. Retrace your steps and go through each piece of information with your recipient, one by one. Take your time, seek clarification, make sure you are satisfied that it's a 'yes' from your recipient before you move on to the next piece of information, particularly if it's related to what you've just said.

You've Given Too Few Pieces of Information to Your Recipient

Sometimes your recipient says 'no' because you haven't gone far enough. If you are describing something that is sensitive or emotional or you're unsure as to its accuracy, you might hold back and hope that the recipient 'gets the gist' without you having to express the point clearly and in full. Don't make them do the work. Find a loving way to tell everything that you perceive from Spirit to avoid this kind of 'no'.

You Interpreted the Information Too Much

If we are working psychically, we often have to interpret information we receive (this should apply less to mediumship because we're aiming for verifiable facts, rather than information that's open to interpretation), but if symbolic information does come through, we can tend to overwork it and interpret it in such a way that the intended meaning is lost.

You've Misunderstood the Person in Spirit

Sometimes we get it wrong. It happens to brain surgeons, Olympic athletes, hairdressers, chefs and parents – and it will happen to you too. If you get the feeling, the sense, that a piece of information you've given isn't quite right, admit your mistake, go back into the power and ask the person in Spirit for clarification. It doesn't have to be a crisis and it doesn't mean you should stop the message.

You're with the Wrong Recipient

If you are getting lots of 'no's in a row, and your communication feels stuck and lacking in energy, it could be that you're trying to give the message to the wrong person. This can happen in public demonstrations and in one-to-one work, if you're reading for a family, group of friends or community who are very close. Signals can get mixed up sometimes. This, again, is why it's so important to present one piece of information at a time, so you can be sure you're giving the message to the right person. If it feels off, trust your feelings. Stop and ask if anyone else can understand the message, or ask the recipient if it feels like the message is for them. It's better that it goes to the right person after a few attempts than a perfectly packaged message goes to the wrong person.

Your Recipient Has Forgotten

I once got the name 'Jean' for a woman in a public demonstration. I asked her if she knew anyone called Jean, either living or in Spirit. I felt I had her mother with me in Spirit. She said she did not know anyone with that name, until her sister nudged her and reminded her that *her own* name was Jean. Receiving a message can be stressful and can cause your recipient to draw a blank. Be patient; give them time to think about it.

Your Recipient Doesn't Want to Hear It

It can happen that your recipient is single-minded about who they want to hear from. It can also happen that they are happy to hear from anyone except the person you have with you. If they don't want to hear it, you can give them the choice about how to proceed. You can explain to them that healing can come from the message and invite them to trust the process, or you can ask them if they'd rather skip that part of the reading. Be honest and patient and check with them. If you truly believe that's what's going on, ask them: is this someone you know, but don't want to hear from?

Your Recipient Isn't Ready to Hear It

If your recipient isn't ready, let it go. Take the 'no' and move on. Some things are not supposed to be said – or at least not right now. Follow your gut instinct here if you sense that they are withdrawing. This is something you'll get to know with practice.

Your Recipient Doesn't Know Yet

This was the case with the story that opened this chapter. My client responded with a 'no' because she didn't yet know that it was a 'yes'. This is when a 'no' is a good thing because it truly proves the existence of Spirit. I could not possibly have got the information from anywhere else but the Great Intelligence because she herself did not know it yet. If you think this is the case for you – and this is something you will get to know through experience; it may be a gut feeling or the message may grow more insistent and vivid as you try to discount or change it in any way – it's OK to ask the recipient to hold the information for future revealing. But do so in this circumstance only. Asking a recipient to 'hold onto' the information when you get a 'no' should not be a default answer – otherwise you lose the opportunity to learn and grow in the ways mentioned above.

I'm sure you can think of many more reasons why you might get a 'no' besides those listed here. Deciding when it's your responsibility to correct a piece of information from Spirit, as opposed to when it's appropriate to leave it with the recipient or to admit your mistake if you realize you're with the wrong recipient is a subtle art. You will get to know why your recipient said 'no', and what you can do about it, through practice, simply by doing it again and again. That's why it's so important not to be afraid of the 'no' and withdraw from your practice, and instead to lean into it and take from it whatever you can. The more you're willing to do this, the better your mediumship will become.

☆ Activation 24 ☆
Collecting 'No's

Becoming too focused on getting a 'yes', to the extent that you're fearful of hearing 'no', can be detrimental to your mediumship. I recommend this exercise to desensitize yourself to the 'no's, the point being to collect as many of them as you can. It should be fun and a bit silly.

Imagine that you are the greatest medium that ever lived, and that you only ever give information that's correct. You are to take on this persona, and begin giving a 'reading' to your 'recipient'. I want you to go for the most specific, the most out-there and most obscure information that pops into your mind. I want you to try to get a 'no' from your recipient. If you give a piece of information that's wrong, you get a point. If you give one that's right, you lose a point. There are two very important considerations to ensure the success of this exercise: first, make sure you do it in a trusted training environment, not with paying clients or unwitting strangers, and ensure that everyone knows the purpose of the exercise, so as not to risk causing offence or confusion. Second, you must still be a medium – you must still try to perceive the information, speak and present the information as you normally would. The only thing that's changed is that you are going for information so specific and obscure that you're *sure* to get a 'no'.

Practise this with a partner or your training group, and sooner or later, there will be laughter at the 'no's. This is a good thing. We want you to begin to associate laughter and light-heartedness with hearing a 'no' from a recipient, so that you become less fearful of it during your readings and demonstrations.

☆ Activation 25 ☆
Simple Storytelling

To be a great medium is to be great at telling a simple, clear and accurate story about your communicator's life. People's lives are a series of interwoven stories and, often, the task of mediumship seems so overwhelming that we don't know how to begin describing a person in

Spirit. Combine that with a fear of getting it wrong and we clam up completely. This exercise will help you get unstuck from a 'no'. It can feel like a lot of pressure to come up with a big, miraculous description of someone in Spirit, but if you focus on simply saying the next true piece of information, it can seem much less daunting to build the message from there.

The next time you're demonstrating or conducting a one-to-one, try the following exercise to move past a 'no', build up your message and cultivate the energy of the communication. Assemble the character of your communicator piece by piece, as though you are carefully completing a complex jigsaw puzzle. And if you take a misstep, that's OK – go back to the last correct piece of information and take it from there.

Regular Confirmation

A note on the practice I'm about to recommend: get into the habit of asking for confirmation after each piece of information you give. I have heard mediums go on and on and on, never stopping to draw breath or ask the client if the information they're giving is accurate. I have also heard tutors teach mediums that their job is 'to tell the client, not to ask questions'. Well, I don't agree with this. I think it's important to ask the client if they're following the description you're giving of the person in Spirit after each and every piece of information for a number of reasons:

- **It confirms accuracy and that the recipient is following what you're saying.** Misunderstandings in communication happen all the time in life, without adding a nonphysical person to the mix! By asking after each piece of information, 'Is that correct?' or, 'Is that true about this person?' or, 'Does that make sense to you?' you're respectfully making sure the recipient is closely following what you're saying, so they can get the very best of the message from their loved one.

- **'Yes' is powerful.** The more your recipient says 'yes' to the information from Spirit, the stronger the energy between you becomes. So if you collect a 'yes' at the end of every sentence, you're helping your energy, the communicators and the recipients to become more unified, thereby creating stronger and clearer communication. If, however, you rabble on and give 20 pieces of information in an elaborate story and then ask, 'Does that make sense to you?' you're only collecting one 'yes' for a lot of work and information. Plus, you don't know which piece of information the recipient is saying 'yes' to, which could lead to confusion.

- **You get the opportunity to fix your mistakes.** Mediumship is not an exact science and we get it wrong sometimes. Collecting a 'no' at the end of a piece of information is just as important as collecting a 'yes', so that you can clearly identify the piece that didn't make sense to the recipient and correct it. Was it your mistake? Did the recipient misunderstand you? Did they simply forget that the piece of information you gave them was relevant? Mediumship is about evidence of survival, and you owe it to your recipient – and to yourself – to show that evidence in the best, clearest, most precise light possible. So get a 'yes' or 'no' for every piece of information you receive in order to learn to grow and become a precise and accurate medium.

Solving the Puzzle

Allow your mind to focus on only the next detail – the next piece of information from Spirit – before moving on. Then, when you do move on, focus on receiving a piece of information that relates to the previous one, so that, again, you're building the impression of the person in Spirit up piece by piece, until the whole picture emerges and you see the person for the first time. The pieces come together in such a way that a deep sense of the communicator comes into view and you no longer have to find the right place for each piece of information – you become aware of the story, the narrative, the person, the emotions, the dislikes, the likes and the love.

Keep it simple, and have patience building up to this.

Correcting a 'No'

Begin your message, and when you receive a 'no', allow your awareness to drop into your heart and stomach. What do you sense there? Why did the recipient say no? Go with your gut feeling and explore this. Is it because of one of the reasons listed previously in this chapter or something else? If you feel that it's up to you to correct the 'no', do so in the following way:

Focus on your dominant 'clair' (*see pages 54–57*) and ask for a piece of information that's true. I am predominantly clairvoyant and clairsentient, so what usually comes for me is how the person most often felt throughout their life or the last feelings they felt. So I simply drop down into my heart and ask: 'What did you feel?' From asking for an impression of how they felt I usually get the sense of whether the person is male or female, who it is they'd like to speak to and what their relationship was like with that person. You can do the same using your own dominant clair.

Tell your recipient exactly what you're sensing in no more than a sentence or two and ask if they understand. Get that confirmation, so you know if you're on the right track or not.

Does the simple piece of information you just received relate to the information the client previously said 'no' to? How so?

In my experience, it takes a lot less energy for all concerned if you proceed to a piece of information related to what you just said than if you try to pick out something at random. Human beings think in stories, and your job, as the medium, is to tell a story your recipient understands. So set the intention to weave the pieces of information into a clear narrative and it will be better understood by your recipient, thereby reducing the likelihood of a 'no' because of confusion or misunderstanding.

When you say to a client, 'I have a man with you in Spirit who is stubborn and won't take the doctor's advice – do you know a man like that in Spirit?' and you get a 'yes', then ask the person in Spirit for the next logical piece: 'What did you have to go to the doctor about?' You may get the impression of high blood pressure, lifestyle choices, cancer or some other condition; simply relay this to your recipient: 'Was he resistant to going to the doctor about his lifestyle choices?' and get a 'yes' or 'no'. If it's a 'yes', proceed to the next piece of information, perhaps asking the person in Spirit, 'What did your family think of you refusing to go to the doctor?' and, again, just describe what you sense, simply and clearly. Keep going in this fashion until you have built up a strong energy between yourself, your communicator and your recipient. At some point, the information will begin to flow much more easily, but don't be afraid to take your time and get it right. Also, there are no hard-and-fast rules as to which question you should ask next, so just go with your gut and think about the next inquiry that seems sensible or important to you. Often, the kinds of things you're guided to ask are also inspired by Spirit or by the recipient to help give them the answers they seek or to help the narrative of their loved one's life in a way they can understand and follow.

In this manner, we build the message up patiently, aiming for accuracy, clarity, impact and evidence that will let our recipients know that their loved ones are safe and well amongst the Great Intelligence. I still use this method in my mediumship to this day. There is the odd time when the energy between me, the communicator and the recipient is so strong that it's like a runaway train and the information just flows through me. But most of the time, I'm patiently putting it together, until enough pieces are in place that I can sense them clearly; then the momentum of the message takes over, and it feels like I'm introducing an old friend I've known for many years.

CHAPTER HIGHLIGHTS

★ There are lots of reasons why you might get a 'no' in response to a piece of information you've given. Whatever that is, resist the urge to jump to the conclusion that you're a bad medium.

★ Treat each 'no' as an opportunity to grow. It gives you a chance to know your mediumship more intimately and do better next time. For this reason, a 'no' is the best gift a client can give you.

★ Asking your recipient to 'hold onto' a piece of information for the future is appropriate sometimes, but it should not be your default response to a 'no', lest you lose the opportunity to grow from it.

★ Build an impression of the person in Spirit piece by piece, like a jigsaw puzzle, until the whole picture emerges and you see the person for the first time.

CHAPTER 11
THE FOYS

I sipped my coffee and stretched, taking off my glasses for a few moments to relieve my eyes. I was studying for my metaphysics exam and had unexpectedly come upon two names I recognized – Robin and Sandra Foy. I never thought for a second that the academic study of the properties of all things would lead me back to mediumship, but lo and behold, it had.

It was six degrees of separation. I was looking at the properties and parts of physical objects, which had led me to professor and philosopher Charlie Dunbar Broad, whose essay on properties was a challenging read. I searched for more of his material online and was amazed to discover that he was a member of the Society for Psychical Research in London and had written many books on psychic phenomena. I ordered one of his ancient, tatty old books online and, as I completed my purchase, the online store suggested I might also enjoy *Witnessing the Impossible* by Robin Foy.

I knew little about Robin and Sandra Foy. I knew that they were two quarters of the Scole group who, through their weekly séances, had witnessed some extraordinary phenomena that seemed to suggest the reality of the Spirit World. Although their experiences were a little out of my area of expertise, the book looked interesting, so I ordered it as well.

The books arrived in the post one lazy Saturday morning and, with nothing better to do, I made myself a pot of hot coffee and set up camp on the sofa for a day of reading with Buckley, the dog, at my side. I freed *Witnessing the Impossible* from its packaging and examined it front and back. It was a huge, heavy hardback, with a dust cover depicting the old Scole house in which the alleged miracles had taken place. I creaked open the brand-new spine and began to read...

Several hours later, as I neared the end of the book, having been unable to put it down, gobbling it up with my eyes, my heart was racing and my eyes were wide with amazement. Never had I thought that the happenings at Scole would be quite so awe-inspiring. Even I, a young woman who had communed with 'dead' people across many years, could scarcely wrap my mind around how and why such happenings took place.

The Scole group were four people who sat in a circle together every week, with the intention of witnessing physical phenomena (that is, external, objective evidence from Spirit, as opposed to evidence communicated through a medium). What happened at Scole is widely believed to be the best evidence that has ever been received that there is a Spirit World. The evidence they received included newspapers materializing out of thin air that were verified as being from the period to which they were dated, but were in pristine condition; photographs and strange images appearing on a roll of film that wasn't in a camera; and seemingly conscious balls of light administering healing to those present. Many people, including scientists, were invited to attend these experiments, and many witnessed these happenings.

One part of me felt that the alleged happenings during the Scole experiments were too incredible, too far removed from what we think we know about reality to be believed. But another part was convinced that they were authentic, not least because some of them were uncannily similar to experiences in my own communion with Spirit. The similarities gave me the sense that the Scole participants and I had accessed the same 'world' – a world that is cohesive and has properties and laws of its own. It was a feeling I couldn't shake.

After reading the book, I visited the Foys' website to get more information and look at some of the amazing pictures of phenomena that had been captured during the experiments. I went to the forum to meet some like-minded individuals and introduce myself, and as I read Robin's post about the rules of the group, I was shocked to see that Robin and Sandra lived in Alicante, Spain, where I was due to go less than a week later.

Right there and then I made the decision that I was going to meet them. I e-mailed Robin, asking if they would allow me to take them for a meal and interview them – they agreed.

The day of the meeting came and I was so excited. A million questions raced through my mind, and I managed to write some of them down. I put on a floaty dress and sandals, and my mum-in-law, who I was visiting in Alicante, offered to drive me to the restaurant where we were to meet. We arrived at exactly the same time as Robin and Sandra and I waved to them as we pulled up. They were bright, cheery and friendly, and there was nothing about their appearance to suggest the extraordinary nature of the lives they led.

We ate, drank and chatted and, after a short time, I was much more relaxed, enjoying my meal and listening to Robin and Sandra talk about their amazing experiences.

If I'm completely honest – sorry, Robin and Sandra, if you're reading this – I was looking, listening and feeling carefully for any sign of fakery, mixed messages, hesitant answers or avoidant body language that would let me know the whole thing was an elaborate ruse, but I detected none of these. I asked them difficult questions, each of which was answered openly, honestly, joyfully, with full eye contact and an amazing amount of detail. We spent several wonderful hours together and I was convinced that some incredible miracle had taken place. I wanted to know their secret. I took a sip of my drink, as I endeavoured to uncover it:

'Why you? Why Scole? Of all the places and times for this miracle to take place, why then and there?'

We explored the possibilities together and I listened intently until Robin said something that really piqued my curiosity. A light bulb pinged in my awareness, and I suddenly felt that I was having a breakthrough – that a new level of understanding was about to unfold, that the secret would be revealed to me. Open-mouthed, wide-eyed and with my fork loaded, suspended in mid-air, I listened as he said:

'When the Scole group was most harmonious, that's when the best evidence came. And when the group became disharmonious, that's when the phenomena dissipated.'

Bingo, I thought.

Defining Harmony

Irrespective of what happened in the Scole experiments, Robin and Sandra Foy gave me a gift of immeasurable value over dinner that balmy evening, when they said that the strongest, most compelling evidence came when the group was at its most harmonious.

I began to explore whether in my own mediumship there was, indeed, a relationship between me feeling harmonious within myself and the quality of my work. I identified that when I was feeling in harmony, I felt a combination of peace, ease, joy, love, enthusiasm, expansiveness, acceptance and freedom.

I began asking myself, *What does it feel like to be disharmonious?* I identified a lack of harmony as a combination of fear, stress, anxiety, frustration, anger, sadness, complacency and apathy.

I became consciously aware of my feelings, looking out for moments when I dropped into disharmony. I frequently asked myself the question: what would bring a greater sense of harmony to this situation? And if an answer came that was within my power to act on, I did so, all the while monitoring if these changes were making any difference to my mediumship.

The search for harmony as a means to better my mediumship led me to stop drinking alcohol, get more exercise, meet new people, heal family relationships, forgive the past, be more generous, be more accepting of generosity towards myself, move house, triple my income, hire a coach (and have such an amazing experience that I trained as one), go on adventures around the world, get engaged to the love of my life and write this book. And with each and every decision I've made to course-correct to harmony, my mediumship has grown deeper, stronger, more open, clear, consistent, energized, healing, compassionate, diverse and joyful. And so I must conclude that increasing feelings of harmony in your life increases the quality of your mediumship.

Muhammad Ali once said, 'The fight is won or lost far away from witnesses – behind the lines, in the gym, and out there on the road, long before I dance under those lights.'

The same is true for your mediumship. Its success happens out there in your daily life, long before you lock souls with your communicator and recipient.

When I think of harmony, I think of music. I think of an orchestra. The most beautiful, harmonious sound is achieved when all aspects of the orchestra come together in a certain way. The strings, woodwind, percussion, and brass each have their part to play. Likewise, the different aspects of your life harmonize with each other when they are each lived in a certain way. In the Activation section of this chapter, I have included an exercise to help you get clarity about which areas of your life could use a little more harmony, and to decide upon what you need to do to create it. You are a unique individual, so many of the actions you need to take will be specific to your life and your situation. I encourage you to explore and examine what living a harmonious life means to you, and how you can create your definition of harmony in your life and mediumship in your own unique and beautiful way. There are, however, a few suggestions I'd like to make as to how you can bring greater harmony into your life, as it relates to your mediumship, because I believe they are universal. I will share these with you now.

Create Harmony by Being Yourself

The more true you are to yourself, the better you'll be as a medium. I'd encourage you to do life, and mediumship, your own way. That I am 'The Medium in Manolos' has nothing, really, to do with shoes. It has to do with bringing my own essence, my own personality, my own style to my work with Spirit. All too often, our work is presented in such a way that causes mediums to stop being themselves, and start being 'platform mediums' instead. They begin to speak unnaturally, using a tone, register and vocabulary that are different from those they would use with their friends. This creates distance between them and their recipients, who can tell a mile away that they are not speaking from their true heart and, in turn, makes the reading more difficult and less impactful.

When you are conducting your mediumship, you are asking both the communicator and the recipient to be vulnerable with you. It is only fair, then, that you join them in that vulnerability, authenticity and intimacy. It is very challenging as a medium, and as a human being, to remain vulnerable when you are afraid, nervous or anxious, and your ego will want to put a wall up to protect you. But if you can work on yourself in the ways offered in this book, such that you know, accept and love yourself, then you will be empowered to turn up for your clients – not behind a wall of stuffy, stilted and impersonal communication, but with real feeling, authentic compassion and true emotion that will make the message from Spirit even more special and impactful.

So if you have a sense of humour – flaunt it. If you have a beautiful and distinctive style – wear it. If you have a way with words – use them. If it's your desire that your mediumship takes place in a sacred, dedicated space – do it. If you truly feel sorrow and compassion for your recipient – show it. Remember, Spirit works best when you are your best self. Spirit doesn't want you to hide when The Medium comes out. Your unique personality is what makes you able to reach certain people in Spirit, and certain recipients in a way that no one else can. Be proud of who you are, and know that Spirit loves you, appreciates you and wants to work with you – the real you. Meet your clients and communicators with that level of honesty and intimacy and your mediumship will soar.

Create Harmony by Caring for Yourself

Self-care is about caring for *all* of you: your mind and your body; your spiritual and material needs. It's about saying what you mean, accepting your range of human emotions, as and when they arise and loving yourself enough to be empowered to feel, release and forgive them.

Self-care can be as profound as attending a silent retreat with a spiritual mentor or as simple as treating yourself to a manicure and afternoon tea. It can sometimes mean tidying your home from top to bottom or leaving it for another day. It isn't about doing or not doing any one particular thing; it's about the intention behind and the motivation for your actions, and the degree of self-love and self-awareness with which you make decisions about what's best for you.

There are two main reasons why I invite you to practise self-care as a means to improve your mediumship and your relationship with Spirit. The first is that you cannot give what you don't possess – Spirit can only work with what you give them, so if you want to be a vessel for messages of love, you must regularly create and surround yourself with the feeling of love. Think of it this way: imagine you have to make an important call and there are two mobile phones on a table in front of you. One of them has a cracked screen, a missing button, a scraped and scratched case and the screen is flickering on and off because the battery is at 2 per cent; the other is shiny and new, in good condition and has a strong signal and full battery. Which phone would you use to make your call?

Often, self-care looks like learning and growth. Invest in yourself – in your mind, your skills and your talents. The more you treat yourself with compassion, love and kindness, the more you'll notice these things flowing throughout your life and your mediumship.

When you know, love and appreciate yourself and your life, you begin to harmonize with the melody of Spirit, which is love. Whether you're the medium or the recipient, if you want a miracle, you have to ready yourself for one. I'm doing everything I can to ready myself by living lovingly in harmony with who I really am, so that I can be lovingly in harmony with Spirit. And I desire the same for you, so that you can be ready for your most miraculous mediumship to move through you, as Spirit works with your loves and strengths.

Create Harmony through a Consistent Devotional Practice

You are distinct from, and yet part of, a creative force that's bigger than you. Throughout this book, I've called it the Great Intelligence, but others may call it God, Spirit, Source, the Universe and other names. It's a good idea to remind yourself of your connection to the Great Intelligence often, and not just when you get up on platform or do a sitting. Get to know Spirit in private, quiet moments: on your yoga mat, in your journal, during your morning stretching and breathing routine, in a hot aromatherapy bath at night...

Across time, I have done all these things. But for me, the best way I know to 'check in' with Spirit is gratitude. There is nothing more powerful to bring you into harmony with the moment than being grateful for the moment. There is nothing better for getting into harmony with your life than intentionally appreciating your life. And there is nothing more spectacular for growing your gifts as a medium than being deeply grateful for and savouring them – especially the challenging bits! In my experience, devotion, little and often, is more beneficial than grand gestures. Being mindful of the blessings in your life throughout the day and whispering 'Thank you' does more for your bond with Spirit than spending a fortune on a weekend retreat as an act of devotion – although that has its place too.

I realized that gratitude was truly working for me as a devotional practice when, one day, I caught myself feeling truly grateful when a client said 'No' to a piece of information I'd given her from Spirit. Quite unexpectedly, I felt enthusiastic and excited by this 'no'. This was a transformational moment for me, as I suddenly understood, having lived in fear of it for many years, what it could actually teach me about the ways in which my mediumship still had room to grow.

Not only is a regular devotional practice in which you check in with Spirit good for your wellbeing, it also means that when you come to give your demonstration or private sitting, you are already intimately connected to Spirit, like loving, old friends.

Create Harmony by Surrendering to the Moment

Giving a demonstration of mediumship or a one-to-one sitting can make you so anxious. I'm more than a decade into my career and I still get butterflies. To be a little nervous is normal – I'm convinced those nerves are the feeling of our bodies coming into harmony with Spirit. But if you are too anxious, too fearful, too worried or unsure when the moment of truth arrives, it can be detrimental to the clarity of your mediumship. So it's important that you are available to be in harmony with yourself, the communicator from Spirit and your recipient when that moment comes, and I have a few suggestions as to how you can do that.

First of all, you need to relax. I know the feeling of pressure when those expectant faces are looking at you, waiting for their miracle, but that pressure won't serve you. It's out of your hands. Spirit is there to the degree that the communicator, you and the recipient are available for it. You're in charge of your part and, as I mentioned earlier, your work needs to have been done consistently, and long before the time of communication. The best thing you can do when it comes to it is to relax and enjoy yourself. If you're anything like me, you live for that moment and feel happiest when in communion with Spirit. So let yourself be there, in communion, and enjoy it.

Focus on being of service. If you're anxious, fearful or freaking out, then your focus has slipped and your ego has been let loose. You come out of harmony with Spirit when you get lost in your own head – in your own fears. Come back. Focus on the other person; focus on Spirit. Think about how blessed each of you will be to participate in this miracle. Think about how much the communication will mean to them and how freeing and joyful it will be to hear from their loved one. Think about giving this person the most loving, attentive and generous part of yourself. Move your focus away from how you look or what people might be thinking or what they'll say afterwards, and focus on enjoying yourself and setting the intention to be sincerely and easily of service to Spirit. Remember that you are there to be of Divine service – this moment doesn't have to be about you and how you perform. I hope you'll see the truth in that, and that it'll bring you some relief.

Now close your eyes and take a deep breath in through your nose, feeling the oxygen travel through your body, stilling and calming you as it does, then breathe out.

When you begin your message, be genuine about what you're receiving and what feels true to you. Say what's really there. If it's one sentence or a single impression, that's OK. A single sentence of sincere truth is better than a grand, made-up story. Don't be afraid of the silence – and don't be afraid to let the information rush forth either, if that's what's truly there. Take your time, feel it out, ask for clarification, be excited and optimistic. Remember to collect those 'yes' and 'no' answers and avoid making them mean anything about you. Be present, be you and you'll be available for the miracle.

☆ ACTIVATION 26 ☆
The Wheel of Harmony

If you're ready to create more harmony in your life, and in your mediumship, it is useful to take stock of where you're starting from, and the wheel of harmony will help you to do just that.

Here's what I want you to do:

You'll notice that the wheel has segments to represent different areas of your life, and that each segment is divided into sections that represent a percentage. Your task is to colour each segment up to the percentage that represents how harmonious you feel in that area of your life. You can colour directly into the book or redraw the circle if you wish, or you can download a digital version of the wheel from my website: www.laurenrobertson. co.uk/mim/wheel. Use any colours you want.

If, for example, you feel that you are 100 per cent harmonious in your love life, you would colour that segment from the centre, up to the outer edge, so that it's completely coloured in. If you are 50 per cent harmonious, colour half of it to represent 50 per cent. If you are 10 per cent harmonious, colour just 10 per cent of the segment and so on. Don't worry about it being perfect, just as long as it represents the percentage you chose.

Do this for each segment.

When you have finished, you'll have a visual representation of what is – and isn't – harmonious in your life right now. Anything above 50 per cent is harmonious. Around 50 per cent is neutral and any segments you have coloured in less than 50 per cent are disharmonious.

Helpful hint: if there are areas of your life that are important to you that are not featured in the wheel, you are welcome to add and consider them too.

Once you have a true visual representation of how harmonious you feel, it's time to dig deeper. The object here, is to flag up areas of disharmony and act to correct them, so that the increased feelings of harmony in your life may be reflected in your mediumship.

So choose a time when you can be undisturbed, grab your journal and answer the following questions for each segment:

- Why did you fill the section up to the percentage you did? What's good and harmonious in that section?

- Why did you only fill the section up to that percentage? What's not perfect yet? What would take you up to 100 per cent?

☆ ACTIVATION 27 ☆
Your Spiritual Practice

Having a spiritual practice simply means spending time feeling close to Spirit, other than in the context of a mediumship message. I feel closest to Spirit when I walk my dog through the Ayrshire countryside, admiring nature in peace and silence. There is no right or wrong way to feel close to Spirit; it is a personal choice. But you will know you're close by the *feeling* you experience. I have devised the following questions to help you identify that feeling, and when you most commonly have it, so that you have a sense of which spiritual practices truly resonate with you and whether you could enrich feelings of harmony between yourself and Spirit/God/your Creator by stepping up your spiritual practice.

In your journal, answer these questions:

- What are you doing when you feel most harmonious and at peace?

- Where can you find one hour per day to dedicate to harmonious activities and your spiritual practice?

- What's missing from your spiritual practice that you need to begin doing? (If you're anything like me, you'll know what it is because the nagging thought to do it keeps coming!)

- What do you need to stop doing that's disharmonious for you at this stage of your life, to make room for more harmonious practices?

☆ ACTIVATION 28 ☆
In the Moment

Remember, when the time comes for communication, you should resist the urge to meditate, beg, plead, bargain with Spirit, freak out, withdraw into yourself, worry about how you look or what the other person is thinking. All you have to do is be there and be available for Spirit. Nothing else.

Relax, put your hand on your heart, focus on your good intentions and say to yourself: 'I'm here, I'm present, I'm available.'

Then simply enjoy yourself, my love. And remember that Spirit is always with you because you are Spirit. To show up and be you and do your best with good intentions in your heart is all you ever need do – let their loved ones take it from there.

CHAPTER HIGHLIGHTS

★ Increased harmony in your life equals increased harmony with Spirit equals amazing results in your mediumship.

★ The more you are true to yourself and do things your own way, the better your mediumship will be.

★ Success in your mediumship happens long before you sit down to work with that client or get up on that platform – it happens in the harmony you create in your daily life.

CHAPTER 12
THIS IS NOT THE END

Congratulations, my dear medium. (I can call you that by now, right?) I'm so thrilled to welcome you to our final chapter. I want to take a moment to acknowledge you and commend you on completing this journey with me. You have shown that you are willing to do whatever it takes to have the clearest, strongest relationship with Spirit, both for yourself and in your capacity as a medium.

You have shown that you are prepared to do what most are not to heal from grief, and to overcome the fear of death and loss, so that you can live as fully and as freely as possible. And, through your mediumship, you will be powerful in helping others to do the same.

You have looked into dark corners where others fear to tread. You have reached up on tiptoes to the back of that dusty old wardrobe in your mind and pulled out memories, beliefs, thoughts and stories that may have caused you anything from a twinge of nostalgia to full-on pain. You have cracked open your heart and let the light in. You have made yourself vulnerable and surrendered yourself to Spirit. You have let go and trusted that you will be carried by the current of the Great Intelligence.

Wherever you choose to go from here, and whatever is happening in your life right now, completing the transformative and challenging exercises in this book is an amazing accomplishment and you should be immensely proud. Spirit is watching. The Universe has witnessed your determination and those in Spirit who need you to speak on their behalf and remind the world that they lived, await your next move.

I want you, my dear medium, to make that next move a great one. I want you to know that anything and everything is possible for you – you were born worthy and deserving of miracles in the eyes of Spirit.

If a 30-year-old, shoe-obsessed gal from Ayrshire, Scotland can travel the world coaching mediums and demonstrating her mediumship, touching lives and writing books, communing with the 'dead' for a living, then absolutely anything is possible. And it is all possible for you.

So whether the next step for you is to begin speaking of your loved one who died, for the first time, with laughter and love in your voice instead of pain and fear... or you're a new medium who's plucking up the courage to do that first reading, that first platform demonstration or to put your hand up and participate for the first time... or you're a seasoned medium, ready to fill your appointment book, demonstrate your mediumship globally, write books and experience the fullness of life with Spirit – I want you to know that all this and more can be yours: your desire contains within it the blueprint for its fulfilment.

As I end this final chapter, I realize that this doesn't have to be a grand, final farewell. That wouldn't be fitting, since you and I both know there are no grand, final farewells. Neither must I make sure that you've got your packed lunch, been to the toilet, got your ticket and packed the kitchen sink for the journey ahead. It's not necessary for me to recap everything for you or to cram in one more exercise – everything is perfect as it is. You are perfect as you are.

And so I will leave you (for now) with this thought:

Our duty as mediums is not just to the dead, but also to the living: to those who have not yet returned to the light – our brothers and sisters who are going through this school that we call life alongside us. So if you're ever in doubt about how to feel the presence of your loved one in Spirit, how to get the communicator's name in your mediumship or how to keep that stream of clients flowing, simply put your hand on your heart and say *we are one.* Act from that knowing, and show kindness, openness and love to a living person. If you take only one thing from the time we have spent together, let it be this: what we do in life, we become in our mediumship.

All my love,

Lauren x

ACKNOWLEDGEMENTS

I'm so grateful to the following people without whom this book would not have been possible:

My darling Gabriel – throughout the writing process, you have truly been an angel by name and an angel by nature. My two fur babies, Buckley and Booboo: your snuggles and head boops lifted my spirits on numerous occasions. My family – Jane, Carly, Lewis, Jamie and the kids – your love and encouragement mean the world to me. Holly Abell and Courtney Cope – through laughter, tears, ups and downs, you've supported me and given so generously of yourselves and your gifts; thank you for being blissfully and purely happy for me. Giovanna Capozza – thank you: at a key moment you went way beyond the call of duty to ensure this book got written. Gina DeVee, Dr Glenn A. Sisk, and all at Divine Living – thank you for showing me that when I have one foot on Earth, and one foot in the Spirit World, those feet are allowed to have Manolos on them. Ally Bhatia, thank you so much for being the best 'video guy' a girl could wish for. To David R. Hamilton PhD and Ali Campbell, thank you so much for taking me under your wings, for your generous support and for seeing something in me before I was able to see it in myself. To Amy Kiberd, Michelle Pilley, Julie Oughton and all at Hay House UK – thank you for making my dream come true. Thank you also to Leonora Craig Cohen and Anne Newman for your invaluable editorial input. I am also so grateful to Charlene Salmon, Pia Osberg and Neale Kelly; I couldn't have written this book without your support.

My thanks to all of you who have invited me to speak at your spiritualist churches or events or into your homes to do readings. Thank you also for joining me in my living room and permitting me precious insight into your lives. Thank you for being so open-hearted and open-minded and allowing me the honour and privilege of speaking on behalf of your loved ones in Spirit.

To my clients, students and those who follow my work: you are my reason for writing this book; thank you for all you have taught me.

From the bottom of my heart, I must thank you, dear reader. Thank you for buying this book and reading my words.

And finally, to each and every soul in Spirit who's entrusted me to deliver your most precious of messages – thank you for allowing me to be the receptacle of your miracle.

ABOUT THE AUTHOR

© Matt Marcus Liengie

Lauren Robertson is a Spirit communicator and transformational coach from Ayrshire, Scotland.

In addition to passionately demonstrating and speaking about mediumship, Lauren specializes in helping mediums and intuitive practitioners achieve excellence and confidence in their work, via transformational coaching techniques, on a one-to-one basis and in groups.

Lauren has served tens of thousands of people in her capacity as a medium and has spoken on UK and international platforms. Her work can be read and listened to online, and she is the host of the 'Higher Power Podcast'.

Lauren holds a MA Hons in English Literature and Philosophy from the University of Glasgow where she spent her time studying the mind and approaches to understanding consciousness.

The Medium in Manolos is Lauren's first book, published by Hay House. Her love for mediumship is, as the title suggests, matched only by her love for designer shoes.

She lives in the West of Scotland countryside with her fiancé and two fur babies.

www.laurenrobertson.co.uk

HAY HOUSE
Look within

Join the conversation about latest products,
events, exclusive offers and more.

 Hay House UK

 @HayHouseUK

 @hayhouseuk

 healyourlife.com

We'd love to hear from you!